Small Treasures

Photo credits: Joan Balzarini, Bob Bernhard, Susan Fox, Isabelle Francais, Peter Gurney, Michael Gilroy, Tony David Jones, Theo Kleefisch, Horst Mayer, Andre Roth, Vincent Serbin, Louise B. Van der Meid, and Terry Wing

Distributed in the UNITED STATES to the Pet Trade by T.F.H. Publications, Inc., 1 TFH Plaza, Neptune City, NJ 07753; on the Internet at www.tfh.com; in CANADA by Rolf C. Hagen Inc., 3225 Sartelon St., Montreal, Quebec H4R 1E8; Pet Trade by H & L Pet Supplies Inc., 27 Kingston Crescent, Kitchener, Ontario N2B 2T6; in ENGLAND by T.F.H. Publications, PO Box 74, Havant PO9 5TT; in AUSTRALIA AND THE SOUTH PACIFIC by T.F.H. (Australia), Pty. Ltd., Box 149, Brookvale 2100 N.S.W., Australia; in NEW ZEALAND by Brooklands Aquarium Ltd., 5 McGiven Drive, New Plymouth, RD1 New Zealand; in SOUTH AFRICA by Rolf C. Hagen S.A. (PTY.) LTD., P.O. Box 201199, Durban North 4016, South Africa; in JAPAN by T.F.H. Publications. Published by T.F.H. Publications, Inc.

MANUFACTURED IN THE UNITED STATES OF AMERICA BY T.F.H. PUBLICATIONS, INC.

Contents

An Introduction to Small Pets

The decision to buy a small animal should not be made on impulse. Choosing the right pet requires careful thought and some research. The information in this book will help you make a good choice by answering questions about how well the pet might fit into your family.

SMALL PETS FOR SMALL CHILDREN

Owning a pet is one of the pleasures of childhood. Besides being fun, it is beneficial. A pet can help teach children respect for other living creatures. Kids learn that a pet is not a toy and that it has needs separate from their own desires—for example, that they should not handle the pet too much and that the pet must be allowed to sleep even when they would rather take it out to play. Pets also allow children to assume responsibility and learn nurturing skills. They help children learn how to be compassionate, how to play gently, and what hurting means. Raising a pet from a young animal to adulthood can be a rewarding experience. Children enjoy the process of discovery that comes from caring for a pet.

For a number of reasons, small animals—with the exception of ferrets for very young children—are ideal pets for children. Children are captivated by their cute looks and interesting habits. These pets do not require much time to care for and are often content to be left alone in their cage for several hours at a time, such as when children are in school. (Most small animals can even remain unattended in their cage over the weekend if they are given extra food and water.) Their small size makes them unintimidating and easy for children to hold and play with.

Even if a child's family owns another pet, such as a dog, having a pet that is theirs alone is an exciting experience for any child. Children are proud of their pets, and by caring for a pet of their own, they develop a lifelong respect for animals. Pets often assume great emotional significance to children and are considered family members.

A little pet can be the source of great pride and endless fascination for a child and will teach her to respect other living creatures.

Parents and children should read about different small animal species *before* shopping for a small pet together. This will avoid impulse buys and ensure that they have selected the perfect pet.

Things to Consider

Children often have their heart set on a certain kind of pet. Parents may prefer that their child keep the same type of pet they had as children. The small animal species sold in pet stores make intrinsically different pets and behave very differently. However, most members of the same species behave predictably.

When shopping for a pet, you will probably have expectations about what your animal will be like, but you may not know which small animal pet will best meet your expectations. Children in particular often expect more from their pets than the animals can give. This can sometimes lead to frustration when the animal does not perform as desired.

You need to know how playful the pet will be and what type of interactions you can expect. Small animals can be very affectionate and enjoy being played with and held. Almost all types of small animal are nocturnal, which means they are asleep during most of the day. In the evening, your pet will be at his cage door, waiting to come out and play. He will make many noises at night when you are asleep—gnawing, cracking seeds, drinking water, and playing with his toys. But these basic facts are not enough to help you make the right choice.

To select the most appropriate type of pet, consider several factors. How much time do you have to devote to the animal's care? Many pets become bored and unhappy if they are never let out of their cage to play. Compared with mice, animals such as rabbits and ferrets are demanding and require a great deal of attention. If you are busy and away from home a lot, choose a pet that does not require much daily interaction, such as a mouse. Do you have time for the daily chores required to care for your pet? Some animals, such as guinea pigs, are messy and must have their cage cleaned more frequently.

Before choosing which pet to share your home with, consider the pet's life span, especially if it will be a child's pet. Children do not have long attention spans. Once the novelty of owning a pet wears off, caring for it can become one more chore to be unenthusiastically carried out. If the child is soon going to become more involved in after-school activities, then a long-lived rabbit (five to eight years) that might sit neglected in his hutch is a poor choice. A better selection might be a rat, which lives only about three years. Some parents are reluctant to get their child a pet because they think the animal's eventual death will be too traumatic. But death is natural, and the years of

Few things are more heartbreaking than the sight of a neglected pet. Even kids with the best intentions may lose interest in a pet after the novelty wears off, and parents must be prepared to take over the pet's care if this happens.

best position to determine whether their child will be able to meet the animal's needs for care and attention.

A child's age and maturity are important factors when deciding which pet to buy. In addition, the size of the pet is important, because this will affect how easily a child can handle the pet and his cage.

Many parents get a pet for a child because they believe it will automatically teach the child about responsibility. This is a mistaken assumption. Parents must use the pet to teach their child about responsibility. Children also need to be taught how to behave around animals.

A common refrain from parents to their children is, "OK, you can get it, but don't expect me to help you care for it." However, depending on the child's age, this can be an unrealistic expectation. While it is understandable that busy parents do not welcome additional responsibilities, an

pleasure and happy memories are usually enough to outweigh the pain at the pet's death.

A Parent's Role

Children learn many positive lessons from keeping pets, including how to care for another creature, compassion, and how to play gently, but parents must realize that they are the guiding force in this learning experience. Naturally, the parents should be the ones to decide whether a child may have a pet. Together, parent and child can consider which small animal pet is best suited to their family's habits and schedule. Parents are in the

Owning a pet can be a great bonding experience for the whole family and is a fun way for children to learn about responsibility.

Preschool-age children must be taught to treat animals gently and compassionately.

With larger pets such as rabbits, children might need help lifting and holding their pet.

animal by itself will not teach a child to be responsible. To a varying extent, a parent must participate in the care of a child's pet. Such assistance might be as little as driving to the pet store to buy fresh food, but it is vital. In many cases, parents must supervise to ensure the safety and health of both the child and pet.

Parents should not give their child tasks that are too difficult. Preschool-age children (three to five years) can help with simple tasks such as pouring pre-measured food into the pet's dish or placing fresh bedding in the pet's cage. Elementary school-age children (six to nine years) can assume more responsibility. For example, they can feed and water their pet and remind their parents when fresh pet supplies are needed. Children ten and older can usually assume almost full responsibility for their small pet, although their parents should still oversee the pet's care to make sure it is not neglected.

Children ten and older can assume almost full responsibility for their pet.

Because young children cannot be expected to care for their pet without some supervision, it helps if a parent is enthusiastic about the pet. Simply by showing an interest in the animal, parents can encourage their child to care for the pet.

Children, and young children in particular, like to play with and occasionally tease their pets. If a small animal struggles while being held, some children tend to squeeze even harder instead of relaxing their hold. Sometimes this rough handling can frighten the animal and cause him to scratch or bite. A parent can help reduce the risk of a bite by showing children how to hold their pets properly and instructing them on what to do should their pet begin to wiggle and scratch (for example, return the pet to his cage). With larger pets such as rabbits, children might need help lifting and holding their pet. Children can also be shown how to open the cage and let the pet come to them rather than pull him rudely from his home. Parents should watch young children when they are playing with the pet.

SELECTING AND CARING FOR A SMALL PET

The best way to avoid disappointment in a pet is to know as much as you can about an animal before sharing your home with him.

An adult should show a child how to handle animals correctly. Using two hands makes the animal feel secure and reduces struggling and scratching. Smaller animals may be placed on a hard surface such as a table, as long as they are prevented from falling.

A healthy small animal should have clear, bright eyes. He should be inquisitive and curious, never fearful or timid.

Knowing ahead of time how an animal interacts with people, the type of care he needs, and other noteworthy characteristics (for example, whether the pet is smelly, destructive, or nips) will help you determine if the pet will meet your expectations and whether you can properly care for the pet.

It is important to remember that there is no such thing as a no-maintenance pet. You cannot take an animal home and forget about him. Your pet depends on you for all his needs.

At the Pet Store

A healthy small animal should have thick, shiny fur. His eyes should be clear and bright and he should look a little plump. When you hold the animal, he should feel solid, not frail. Do not choose an animal that is listless, has runny eyes, a runny nose, a rough or thin coat, lumps, or scabs. Dirty, matted fur near an animal's tail could be a sign of diarrhea. A healthy pet is active and curious. A good choice is an animal that is inquisitive and investigates your hand when you place it in the cage. Do not choose an animal that runs and hides, struggles frantically, or is aggressive and tries to bite. Never buy an animal that bites, because this is typically an incurable trait.

Choose a pet from a clean, uncrowded cage. Animals that come from a dirty, crowded environment are less likely to be healthy. Always pick a young animal, because it will be easier to tame and will most likely live longer than an older animal. Be aware that a female might be pregnant if she was not separated soon enough from the males.

After selecting a pet, be sure to ask the pet store employee how to hold it properly. It is important that you are comfortable handling your pet before you leave the pet store.

Bringing Home Your New Pet

When you first bring your pet home, he might be frightened or nervous. Let him settle down and get used to his new home before you play with him. This may take a couple of days. Use this time to think of a name for your pet to help you tame and train him. Your pet will learn to associate his name with feeding time and playtime. The more you play with your pet, the happier and friendlier he will be.

Small pets like regular feeding and playing times. You will learn how your pet behaves when he is frightened or excited, how he reacts to new situations, and what it means when he assumes different postures. Knowing his normal behavior will help you recognize when your pet might be sick. Any changes in his behavior, such as lack of interest in playing or eating, could mean he is ill and that you should consult a veterinarian immediately.

Housing

Depending on the type of pet you buy, you will need to house him in a wire cage or a glass or plastic aquarium. His house must be escape-proof. A wooden cage is not recommended, because your pet may chew through the wood and escape. Also, wooden cages are difficult to keep clean, because they tend to absorb urine and other odors. Always buy the largest cage you can afford.

If you choose a glass or plastic aquarium, keep in mind that this type of housing is not as well ventilated as a wire cage. Although such cages are beneficial because they are not drafty, they can allow ammonia gas to build up to uncomfortable levels. You must be vigilant in keeping such a cage clean.

Cage Placement

Do not place the cage near a heating or air conditioning vent, a drafty window, or in direct sunlight. Do not leave any items such as clothing or papers on or near your pet's cage, because anything that can be pulled into the cage will be chewed, and some materials are a hazard to the pet's health.

Place your pet's cage in an area where you can enjoy him. Make the cage a pleasant and intriguing part of a room. Set it on a dresser or a table. Do not place the cage on the floor. The disturbance from other pets and people walking by can frighten your pet. Also, the temperature near the floor is often cooler than on a dresser or table. The garage is an unhealthy location for your pet and he is more likely to be forgotten there. A pet should be part of the family, not banished from it.

Bedding

All small animals need bedding in their cage. Bedding is used to absorb moisture, reduce odors, and provide a warm, dry place for your pet to sleep. Wood shavings made of aspen and pine or those treated with chlorophyll work well, as does bedding made from recycled paper. Other sophisticated bedding products are available that help to

A 10- or 20-gallon aquarium is a good home for many small pets. When you first bring your pet home, give him a few days to settle in before you try to handle him.

Many colorful, expandable cages for small pets are available in pet stores. Make sure to buy the largest cage you can afford—there's no such thing as a cage that's too big.

control or eliminate odor. The latter types are more expensive, but they can make it more pleasurable to own a small pet because they will smell better.

Cedar shavings are not recommended, because they cause respiratory problems in some small animals. Do not use newspaper—the ink will make your pet dirty. Small animals also like to burrow through and eat fresh hay. Some animals, such as hamsters, need nesting material, which they shred and make into a sleeping nest. Pet stores sell nesting material, or you can use paper towels.

Accessories

Always place your pet's food in a dish. Use a gravity-demand water bottle to give your pet fresh water. These bottles are sold in pet stores. In case the bottle leaks, do not place it over your pet's food dish. Do not use an open dish to provide your pet with water. The water could spill, and your pet will make the water dirty by filling the dish with his bedding and food.

All small animals need a nest box in which to sleep. This "bedroom" also gives your pet a safe hiding place to retreat to away from loud noises and any disturbing activity outside his cage. A nest box can be made from things found around the house—for example, an empty milk carton—or you can buy one at a pet store. A variety of types are sold, including those that are made to satisfy a small animal's natural instinct to chew, such as fruit-flavored cardboard tunnels, huts made from natural plant fibers, and wooden blocks that a pet hollows out. Other kinds are less destructible and are made of ceramic or hard plastic.

Most small animals will enjoy playing with almost anything you put in their cage. Many wooden toys made for parakeets and parrots are safe to use with your small furry pet. Do not crowd your pet's cage with too many toys—alternate them instead.

Small animals will enjoy playing with almost any toy you provide, whether store-bought or homemade.

Cleaning

No matter how much a pet grooms himself, if the cage is dirty, the animal will not be able to keep himself clean-smelling. A small pet's cage will smell only if it is not cleaned often enough. The more animals kept in a cage, the more often the cage will have to be cleaned. Some small animals need to have the bedding in their cage replaced every other day and some only need it changed every seven to ten days. Many small animals use a corner of their cage for a bathroom. The bedding in this area can be replaced every day or so to prevent odor.

At least once a week, thoroughly clean your pet's home. If necessary, wash the cage with warm soapy water. Be sure to rinse and dry it thoroughly. Replace the nest box as needed. If you play with your pet while you clean his home, cage cleaning will not be a dreary chore.

The smell from a pet's cage is one of the most common complaints of small animal owners. A small animal's droppings do not smell bad, but the urine can develop a pungent smell from ammonia. Ammonia is a severe irritant and is detrimental to the health of animals. No pet should be housed on dirty, wet bedding. But, in between cleaning, bedding with odor-masking agents (such as chlorophyll in shavings), the newer, innovative bedding products designed to control or eliminate odor, or other odor-control products can be used to minimize the smell. However, no odor-control product can solve the problem of too many animals in a cage or not replacing the bedding often enough.

Feeding

Feeding small pets is easy, because quality prepared food mixes are sold for every kind of small pet. Most small furry animals like to nibble on food throughout the day and night, so be sure your pet always has food. If you feed him treats of moist food, remember to remove any uneaten moist food or feed him only as much as he can eat in one sitting. Hard foods and chew sticks are necessary, because a rodent's teeth are constantly growing and your pet needs to keep his teeth trim.

Do not feed a small pet through the wires of his cage. Otherwise, anything (including a finger) that is

Never feed a small pet through the wires of his cage. If you do, anything you stick through the wires in the future will be bitten, including your fingers.

A small animal's diet should consist of a wide variety of seeds, fruits, and vegetables. For added nutrition, many seed diets are fortified with vitamins, minerals, and amino acids. Supplemental products are also available to keep your pet healthy. Photo courtesy of Sun Seed Company, Inc.

Ferrets are one pet that can be trained to use a litter box. Place the box against a wall so that your pet is likely to encounter it as he plays in the house.

Your pet not only needs a well-balanced diet but exercise as well. Exercise treats are consumable toys that encourage pet activity and help prevent pet boredom. Photo courtesy of Sun Seed Company, Inc.

poked through the cage bars might get nipped. Children should be told to open the cage door to offer a treat. They should also wash their hands before handling the pet in case any food smells on their hands entice the pet to bite, and they should wash their hands after handling the pet as well.

Exercise

Part of the fun of owning a small furry pet is taking him out of his cage to play. Many people allow their pets to explore and play in the room in which their cage is kept. Before doing this, you must "pet-proof" the room. Pick up "edible" items off the floor. Small pets can eat and dig up potted plants or chew electrical cords, papers, and books. Close up nooks and crannies so that your pet does not escape. Place your pet's cage on the floor and let him begin his explorations from his home. That way he always knows where he can run to be safe. Never let your pet loose in a room without supervising him.

Be aware that your pet might leave droppings in the room as he explores. However, some small animal pets, such as rabbits and ferrets, can be litter-trained. Place some of your pet's dirty bedding, including his droppings, in a kitty litter box with low sides or in a small-animal litter pan. Let your pet loose to play in the "proofed" room containing the litter box. Remember to supervise him at all times. Place the litter box against the wall so that your pet is most likely to encounter it. Also, put your pet in the litter box during play sessions so that he knows the box is there.

Ferrets

The playful ferret is the domesticated descendent of the European polecat. Ferrets have been raised in Europe since Roman times and were imported into the United States in the 1870s. Ferrets were used as hunting animals, trained to go into holes to drive out pests such as rabbits and rats. If properly introduced, ferrets can often get along well with dogs and cats, but not with other small animals, such as hamsters, rabbits, and guinea pigs.

The domestic ferret belongs to the same scientific family as skunks. Members of this family are known for the strong, unpleasant odor they can discharge from scent glands located near their anus, although the adult neutered ferret is unable to do this.

DESCRIPTION

The ferret has a long, slender body that enables it to move with ease through the burrows and tunnels where its prey lives in the wild. It has small ears, a whiskered nose, and five toes on each foot. Nearly half of its body length is made up of its long, furred tail. Ferrets are full-grown when they are about six months old.

VARIETIES

Albino and sable are the two basic ferret colors. Sable ferrets come in different shades of black, brown, gray, and chestnut. The feet and tail of both the albino and sable are of a darker color than the body.

Ferrets are playful, inquisitive animals that require nearly as much attention as a cat or dog in order to thrive.

Because of their strong-smelling scent glands, skunks and ferrets are both grouped into the scientific family *Mustelidae*.

FEMALE AND MALE

Female ferrets are called *jills* and male ferrets are called *hobs*. Females usually weigh between 1 and 2 pounds and are between 12 and 15 inches in length. Males are usually larger than females. They weigh between 2 and 3 pounds and are about 20 inches long.

HOW MANY?

Ferrets can be kept alone, but they do like company. If you start off with one ferret, you can always get him a friend at a later time. As long as you gradually introduce the new ferret to your first ferret, there should be few problems. However, you will probably need another cage for your second ferret. Usually, one ferret will be dominant over the other.

AS PETS

Ferrets are affectionate, playful, and curious. They become very tame if bought young and handled often.

The ferret's long, slender body enables him to move easily through the underground burrows and tunnels where his prey lives in the wild.

Ferrets are nocturnal, but they can learn to switch to a daytime schedule. However, carefully consider whether a ferret is the right pet for you. Ferrets are one of the most interesting small pets, but they are nearly as demanding as a dog or cat. Because ferrets live between five and seven years, they are a long-term commitment.

A ferret will be like a kitten or puppy throughout its life. Like a kitten, a ferret is inquisitive, adventurous, and intelligent. Just like a puppy needs a daily walk, a ferret needs playtime each day outside of his cage. This type of commitment is much greater than that required by a guinea pig or hamster.

You must supervise your ferret when he is playing outside his cage. Ferrets like to put things in their mouths. Your pet might swallow something, such as a piece of foam from your couch, which could cause an intestinal blockage and lead to death. All rooms a ferret explores must be "ferret-proofed."

While ferrets make good pets, ferret ownership requires you to be responsible. Many organizations devoted to ferrets do not recommend ferrets for families with children younger than five years of age. Even if they are one person's pet, they are still considered the entire family's pet. When ferrets are playing outside their cage, they have the opportunity to interact with all family members, including very young children.

LIFE SPAN
5 to 7 years

Many ferret lovers find that ferrets are so much fun, they can't stop at just one—they need one in every color!

Ferrets are one of the most interesting small animals, but they are quite demanding and live for five to seven years. Make sure this is the right pet for you.

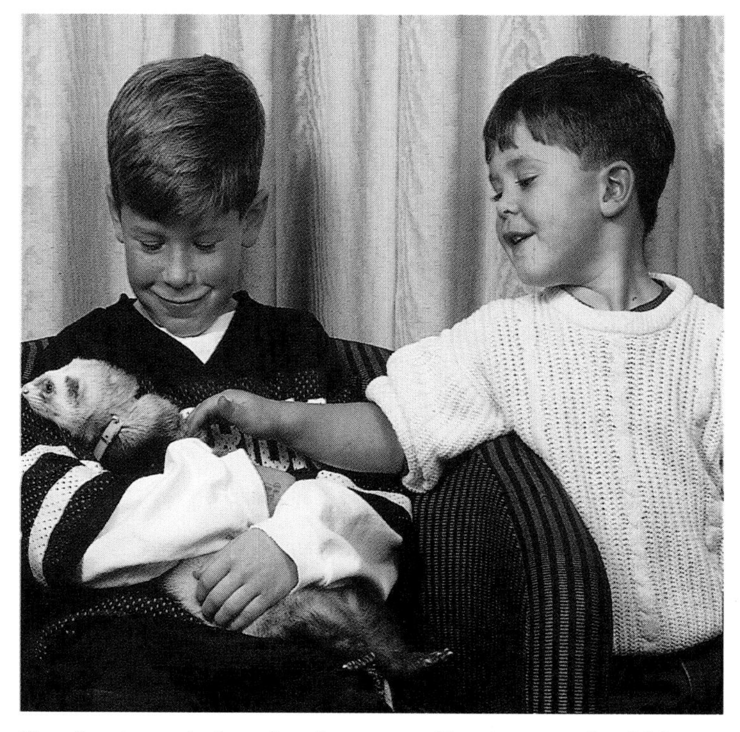

Many ferret organizations do not recommend ferrets as pets for children younger than five years of age. Even tame ferrets can be hard for a young child to handle, and some ferrets are nippy.

Handling a ferret frequently is the best way to make him docile and affectionate. Older children should always be supervised when they interact with their pets.

HANDLING

While your ferret is young, play with him often. Doing so will make your pet more docile and affectionate. Just like a puppy, a young ferret might nip. You must teach your ferret that biting is unacceptable by saying once, in a firm tone, "No!" and tapping him on the nose with your index finger.

Young children do not know their own strength and do not know how to hold animals. They can accidentally hurt a ferret, and the ferret could respond by biting. Young children should never be allowed to handle your pet without adult supervision. Even though your ferret is tame and friendly, never leave a baby or a small child alone with a ferret. A ferret has sharp teeth and a strong grip.

CHOOSING

Choose a healthy, friendly ferret, preferably one that is curious and gentle. Expect young ferrets to play-bite, but do not choose one that nips and hangs on without letting go. If the ferret you want is not already descented and neutered, you will have to pay to have a veterinarian perform this procedure.

Please note that it is legal to keep ferrets in most states, but not all. In addition, some cities and counties have regulations governing the ownership of pet ferrets. Generally, if ferrets are sold in the pet stores where you live, they are legal to own.

HOUSING AND ACCESSORIES

Ferret cages are available in many styles and sizes. The cages, which are made of wire mesh, come in single, double, and triple-story designs. No matter what style the cage is, it must be spacious. One to two ferrets can be kept in a cage measuring 36 in. long x 18 in. wide x 18 in. high. Ferrets are active animals, and their cage should be large enough for separate sleeping, feeding, and litter box areas. Ferrets also need sturdy cages, because if a ferret can escape, he will.

The cage door must always close completely and securely so that the ferret can't get his head stuck in the door. If necessary, fasten the cage door with a clip.

Ferrets like to be a part of their family's activities, so a good location for their cage is often the living room. Be sure to keep your pet's cage out of drafts, because ferrets are susceptible to colds and respiratory illnesses.

Most ferret experts recommend that you place paper or pelleted bedding in the cage tray *below* the wire screen. Ferrets kept directly on their bedding sometimes eat it and become constipated. Ferrets are clean animals and should be trained to use a litter pan, which will make cage cleaning easier.

Pelleted litter made from recycled paper or plant fiber should be used in the litter pan, not clay or clumping litter. Use a litter scooper to remove the droppings each day. You must keep the pan clean or else your ferret might stop using it. Give your pet a small ferret bed or a hammock in which to sleep. Wash your ferret's bed once a week.

FEEDING

Ferrets are carnivorous and need a diet that is high in animal protein (about 36%) and fat (22%) and low in fiber. Prepared foods madc especially for ferrets are available. Chicken and/or poultry by-product meal or whole chicken meat should always be the first ingredient of a quality ferret food, followed by rice flour or

Ferrets are very active, and their cages should be spacious. The cages pictured contain a variety of accessories and toys along with separate feeding, sleeping, and litter box areas—an ideal setup for these rambunctious animals.

It's important to feed your ferrets food that is designed just for them and their special nutritional needs. The food you choose should have high palatability and high digestibility, be made from animal protein, and contain only a small amount of fiber. Photo courtesy of Performance Foods, Inc.

A bath with ferret shampoo every other week will help control your ferret's natural odor.

brewers rice, animal fat, and other quality protein sources such as whole eggs. Grains should not be near the top of the list. Avoid foods with fish as a main ingredient—these are not appropriate ferret foods even if they are labeled as such.

Ferrets have a fast metabolism and eat small meals throughout the day. Your pet should always have food in his dish. Treats can include oat, corn, or rice cereals. Provide fresh water in a water bottle.

SPECIAL NEEDS

Ferrets wash and groom themselves every day, but they still have a natural musky odor because of their skin and scent glands. This odor is stronger in a ferret that is not neutered. Most ferrets that are sold in pet stores are both neutered and descented. Even so, a pet ferret will still have an odor because his skin glands cannot be removed.

A bath with ferret shampoo every other week will control a ferret's scent and help keep him clean. You will also need to trim your ferret's nails about once a month. The area around your pet's cage will always have a slightly musky odor.

Buying a neutered ferret is always preferable to one that is unneutered. Besides reduced odor, neutered ferrets are calmer and cannot breed. It is especially important to buy a neutered female ferret, since a female that is not spayed can develop an irreversible and fatal condition if she is not mated when in heat.

Ferrets need annual visits to a veterinarian. They need to be vaccinated against canine distemper and rabies, and annual booster shots are necessary to provide continuous protection.

BREEDING

Female ferrets are ready to breed at an age of approximately six months. Both females and males are only capable of breeding at certain times of the year, and the peak breeding season is usually between April and May. A pregnancy lasts about 42 days, and a litter averages between 5 and 8 kits. The kits are born blind and deaf and begin to eat soft foods at about three weeks of age. Between five and eight weeks of age, they will be completely weaned.

Gerbils

The 81 known species of gerbil are found in desert areas throughout Africa, parts of Europe, and across Asia into China. The Mongolian gerbil, the species kept most often as a pet, comes from the deserts and plains of Mongolia and other provinces of China. Very hot summers and very cold winters are typical of this gerbil's natural habitat. Adaptations such as tunneling, foraging at night, storing food, and deriving water metabolically from the foods they eat help gerbils survive in the desert environment. A Japanese scientist first captured gerbils for use as laboratory animals in 1935. From Japan, they were brought to the United States in 1954. Because they are gentle and easy to care for, gerbils eventually became popular pets.

The nocturnal gerbil has been a popular pet since the late 1950s. Gerbils are gentle, cute, lively animals that are easy to care for.

DESCRIPTION

Wild gerbils are colored so that they blend into their desert habitat. The dense fur on their back is a golden sandy color, and the fur on their belly is pale gray. Like a kangaroo, gerbils have long muscular hind legs that enable them to hop and leap quickly. Their front legs are shorter and are used to hold food and dig. In the wild, gerbils warn each other of approaching danger by drumming their hind feet on the ground. Even though their ears are small, gerbils have acute hearing. Their large eyes help them to see when foraging at night.

Gerbils measure about nine inches in length, including their long, fur-covered tail, which helps them keep their balance when they sit up and

Gerbils are about nine inches long, including their long, furry tail. Their golden, sandy color helps camouflage them in their native desert habitat.

This ivory gerbil is just one of the many color varieties available. Others include albino, black, golden, and gray.

helps them to leap and turn when pursued by a predator. If a gerbil is grabbed by the black tuft at the tip of his tail, he will lose the skin, exposing the vertebrae, and the tuft will not grow back.

VARIETIES

Besides the standard wild agouti color, other color varieties such as albino, black, golden, cream, and gray have been developed. The eye color is either black or red. Mutations in coat length and texture have not appeared, although they might emerge or be developed in the future. Other species of gerbil, such as the Egyptian gerbil, are occasionally offered for sale. This species is smaller than the Mongolian gerbil and also makes a good pet. Some of the other gerbil species are called jirds.

FEMALE AND MALE

Male gerbils are larger than females. Young male gerbils can be differentiated from females by the dark-colored scrotum located near the base of their tail.

HOW MANY?

Gerbils should be kept in pairs. A gerbil kept by himself will be unhappy and will not thrive. A mixed pair (that will, naturally, produce young) or two females get along best. Males tend to fight as they get older. Buy two young gerbils at the same time so they can grow up together. Adult gerbils (about 12 weeks old) are territorial and will fight if another gerbil is introduced into their home. If raised together, though, a pair of gerbils will form a lifelong bond. They will groom each other, play, and curl up to sleep together.

AS PETS

Gerbils are cute, easy to care for, and practically odorless. Even though they are lively and agile, gerbils are docile, gentle

Gerbils are happiest when kept in pairs. In the wild, they are social animals and do not thrive by themselves.

pets. Unlike many other small animals, they are not timid and nervous. Gerbils will eagerly explore your hand or anything else put near them. Instead of running away from something unknown, inquisitive gerbils will advance and investigate. In new situations, a gerbil will stand on his hind legs, using his tail for assistance, and sniff the air. Tame your gerbils by placing a food treat in the palm of your hand and encouraging them to climb onto your hand.

Gerbils have many interesting behaviors. They communicate with each other by squeaking and thumping their back legs during courtship, play, and when alarmed. Gerbils are even-tempered and not easily provoked to bite. However, if they feel threatened or frightened, they might stomp their hind leg as a sign that they will bite if you do not stop your threatening behavior.

In the wild, gerbils are active at twilight (crepuscular), but domesticated gerbils alternate periods of activity with sleep throughout the day and night. Their favorite pastime is digging and burrowing through the bedding in their cage.

Gerbils should be allowed some supervised playtime outside of their cage. Watch them closely. Gerbils can run fast and may be difficult to catch. Most loose gerbils, however, will explore a room and will not hide. They will return to their cage or your hand if tempted by a treat. Cardboard tubes to climb through, wooden toys and fruit tree branches to gnaw and climb on, and a solid-frame

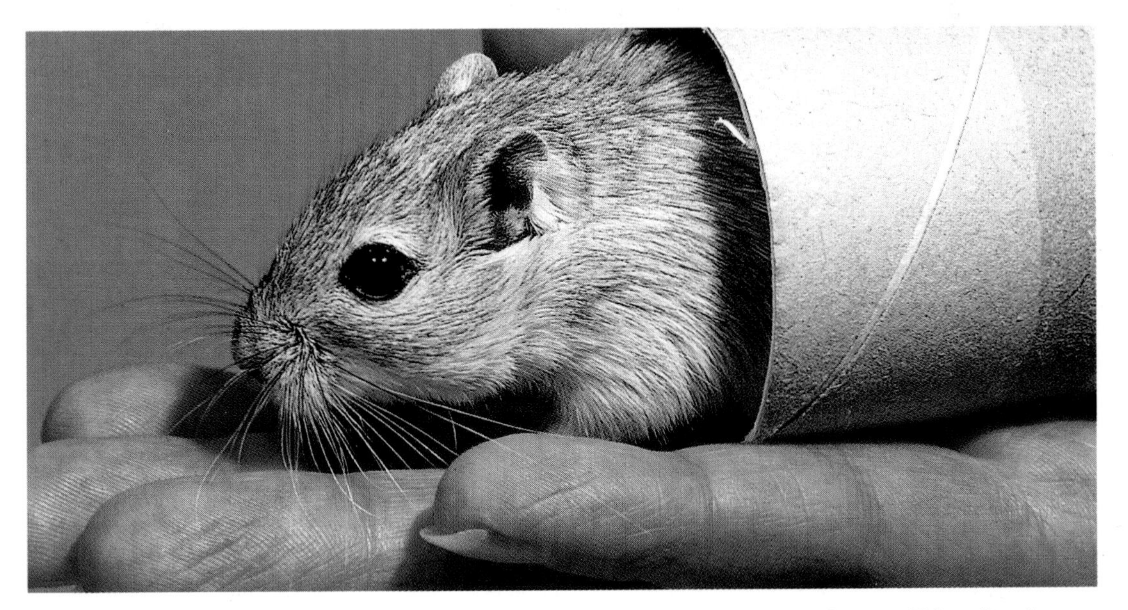

No matter what you put in front of them, gerbils are always willing to explore something new. This trait makes them lots of fun to play with.

This gerbil's owner has provided him with a nearly ideal cage environment, except for one thing—wire-mesh exercise wheels are a no-no for gerbils and other animals with long tails. The tail may get caught between the bars, and the animal could be badly injured. Provide your pet with a solid-frame wheel for maximum safety.

exercise wheel (not wire mesh) to run on will give your gerbils hours of playtime.

Gerbils have almost no odor. Because they evolved in the desert, they drink very little water and excrete only small amounts of urine and small, hard droppings. Cleaning their cage every 10 to 14 days is usually adequate, but you should clean the cage more frequently if needed.

Wild gerbils take dust baths to help keep themselves clean. Pet gerbils also like dust baths. It is very entertaining to watch gerbils take a dust bath. You can use chinchilla dust (usually volcanic ash) or bird gravel for this purpose. Use a container deep enough to hold about a half inch of dust and large enough so that the gerbils can somersault and flip around in the dust. A glass or hard plastic container with sides about two inches high works well. Place the dust bowl in the cage for a short time every few days. Replace the dust after two or three baths.

LIFE SPAN
3 to 5 years

HANDLING

Pick up your gerbil by letting him climb onto your hand or by scooping him up under his belly. Gerbils are frightened when a hand descends down over their back, so always put your hand in the cage palm up, lower it to the bottom of the cage, then move it toward your gerbil. Practice picking up your gerbil in his cage before taking him out. Gerbils are nimble and will often try to get away, so hold the base of your pet's tail (not the tip!) with one hand and cradle his body in the palm of your hand. Do not turn him over on his back and expose his belly. This posture makes gerbils (and most animals) feel vulnerable, and they will become upset and struggle frantically to right themselves.

CHOOSING

Buy gerbils when they are between four and eight weeks old or about two to three inches in body length. Select gerbils that are bold and inquisitive. A gerbil that climbs onto your hand will make a good pet.

Please note that it is not legal to keep gerbils as pets in

This four-week-old Canadian White Spot gerbil is at the perfect age to become someone's new pet. Young animals are easier to tame and handle.

California. The California Department of Fish and Game has banned gerbils because of concerns that if gerbils become established in the wild, they could damage crops and displace native wildlife.

HOUSING AND ACCESSORIES

A 15- or 20-gallon aquarium with a secure wire-screen cover is the best choice for housing gerbils. Because gerbils can jump right out of an aquarium, their cage must always be covered.

Gerbils spend a lot of time digging and kicking bedding and food around their cage, so an aquarium will keep the area around their cage clean. If you use a wire cage, place it inside a kitty litter pan to catch the material that spills out. Provide a deep layer of shavings, about four inches, inside their cage so they can dig and burrow.

Gerbils prefer to sleep in a nest box, which you can make from an old cereal box or other household item or buy in a pet store. Give your gerbils items to play with, such as cardboard tubes and fruit branches. Gerbils will chew on cage furniture, so be sure it is safe. The greater the variety of toys, the more fun your gerbils will have and the more fun they are to watch. Provide your gerbils with toys designed for hamsters and mice, such as tunnels and ladders.

A large aquarium is the best choice for housing gerbils, because they like to dig and kick food and bedding around their cage. They don't eat or drink much, but food and water should always be available.

FEEDING

Gerbils are herbivorous (they eat plants, seeds, and nuts), although some individuals like to eat an occasional invertebrate, such as a mealworm. Packaged foods for gerbils contain all the nutrients your pets need to remain healthy. A gerbil will only eat about a tablespoonful of food a day, but he should always have food available. Water should always be available even though gerbils do not drink much. Give daily treats of small, well-washed pieces of vegetable and fruit. Do not feed too much at one time—this will give a gerbil diarrhea. A handful of cubed or loose hay will provide needed fiber. Dog biscuits are favorite treats, as are many of the treats marketed exclusively for small animals.

SPECIAL NEEDS

Gerbils love sunflower seeds and other fattening nuts. Give your gerbils these fatty foods in moderation, because they are prone to obesity.

BREEDING

Gerbils prefer to select their own mates and sometimes reject potential mates. Their age at first breeding is 10 to 12 weeks. After a gestation period of 25 to 28 days, baby gerbils are born pink and hairless, with their eyes closed. Males help somewhat in rearing their young, which are weaned after 21 days. Usually, 4 to 6 gerbils are born in a litter, but as many as 12 gerbils in one litter have been reported.

Guinea Pigs

Guinea pigs, also known as cavies, were first domesticated centuries ago by South American Indians, who bred them for their prized meat. Sailors returning from their conquests in South America introduced the guinea pig to Europe in the 16th century.

Wild guinea pigs live in colonies in grasslands on the lower slopes of the Andes mountains. They do not dig their own burrows. Instead, they seek shelter in rock outcrops and abandoned burrows dug by other animals. They warn each other of danger by whistling and squealing.

DESCRIPTION

Guinea pigs are short, stout, tailless animals with bellies that touch the ground. They have large heads and appear to have no neck. A full-grown guinea pig is about seven to ten inches long and weighs between two and two-and-a-half pounds. Guinea pigs are not agile and acrobatic. They have short legs and do not jump, climb, or sit up. Instead of holding food in their paws, they eat with all four feet on the ground. Their front feet have four toes, while their hind feet have only three toes.

VARIETIES

At least 13 breeds of guinea pig are recognized. Guinea pigs can be classified by coat type into three varieties. The smooth, short-haired (or American) guinea pigs have dense, sleek hair. The rough-haired guinea pigs (or Abyssinians) have tuftlike rosettes of coarse hair all over their body and a ridge of hair along their back. The

Guinea pigs are small, plump, tailless animals that have been domesticated for centuries. They make great pets for children.

long-haired guinea pigs (or Peruvians) have long silky hair that grows down to the ground. Guinea pigs come in a variety of colors including solid black, cream, chocolate, and golden, and in a variety of patterns such as Dutch (a white body with a pattern of one or two colors), Himalayan (a white body with colored points—nose, feet, and ears), tortoiseshell, and spotted dalmatian.

Guinea pigs are affectionate and very rarely bite. Once they are tame, they enjoy sitting in their owners' laps to be petted.

FEMALE AND MALE

A female guinea pig is called a sow and the male is called a boar. Males are slightly larger and a little less shy than females. If you want more than one guinea pig, get two females, because two males will probably fight when they get older.

HOW MANY?

A guinea pig can be kept by himself if you have plenty of time to play with him. Otherwise, buy two young guinea pigs, because they are sociable and like to have companions.

Three varieties of guinea pig are available. A short-haired, or American, guinea pig is pictured with a long-haired, or Peruvian, guinea pig. The other variety, Abyssinian guinea pigs, have tuftlike rosettes of coarse hair all over their bodies.

AS PETS

Guinea pigs are friendly, gentle animals and are easy to care for. They are good pets for children because, once tame, most will sit calmly in a lap to be cuddled and petted. Affectionate animals, guinea pigs become attached to their owners and look forward to regular playtime. Guinea pigs make good classroom pets. They very rarely bite and, unlike other small furry animals, guinea pigs are active mainly in the daytime.

Initially, guinea pigs are nervous and timid. When you put your hand in their cage, they squeal and run around wildly. Yet with gentle handling, they settle down quickly and are easy to tame and hold. A piece of carrot or apple can help you make friends more quickly.

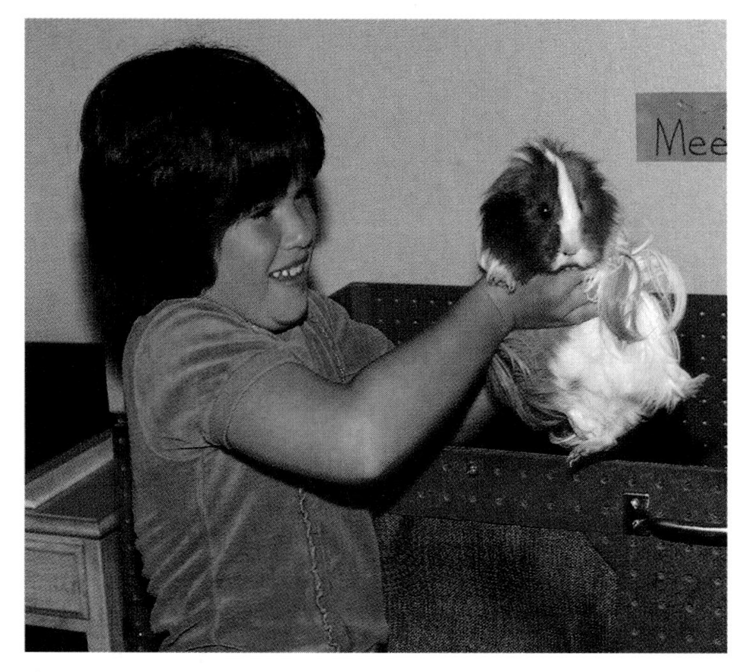

Many elementary school teachers have discovered that guinea pigs make excellent classroom pets, particularly because they are active in the daytime.

As with most animals, abrupt movements and sudden noises will frighten them.

Guinea pigs are very talkative. They make a variety of whistles, squeals, and grunts when excited, hungry, or afraid. Your guinea pig will learn to recognize you and will squeak happily at your approach. At mealtime, he will whistle especially loudly. If you imitate your guinea pig's whistles, he will answer you.

A guinea pig can be amusing inside his cage. One moment your guinea pig might be resting on all four feet, and then suddenly he will pop into action. Bouncing and jumping up in the air, your pet will run in circles, pause, shake his head, twitch, then spring into action and spin about the cage yet again. This delightful behavior is sometimes called "jigging" or "popcorning" and is the sign of a happy guinea pig.

Guinea pigs are happiest when they are allowed to play outside their cage on a daily basis (or at least every other day). Construct an indoor playpen for them where it is safe for them to run and play, or buy one of the plastic enclosures sold especially for this purpose.

Guinea pigs are one of the messier small animals. They spend most of their day nibbling and, as a consequence, they produce a lot of droppings. Although one corner of the cage is often used as a bathroom area, guinea pigs also scatter

Guinea pigs are very messy, and you will have to clean your pet's cage frequently in order to keep him happy and healthy.

droppings throughout their cage, which means more work to keep their cage clean. You will need to clean their bathroom area every few days.

LIFE SPAN

3 to 8 years

HANDLING

Guinea pigs are not surefooted animals. Protect them from falling or jumping, which could seriously injure or even kill a guinea pig. Pick up your guinea pig by slipping one hand underneath his belly, and place the other hand over his shoulders so that he cannot wiggle and fall. Hold your pet by supporting his rear end with one hand and his front paws with the other hand. Cradle your pet next to your body for extra security in handling.

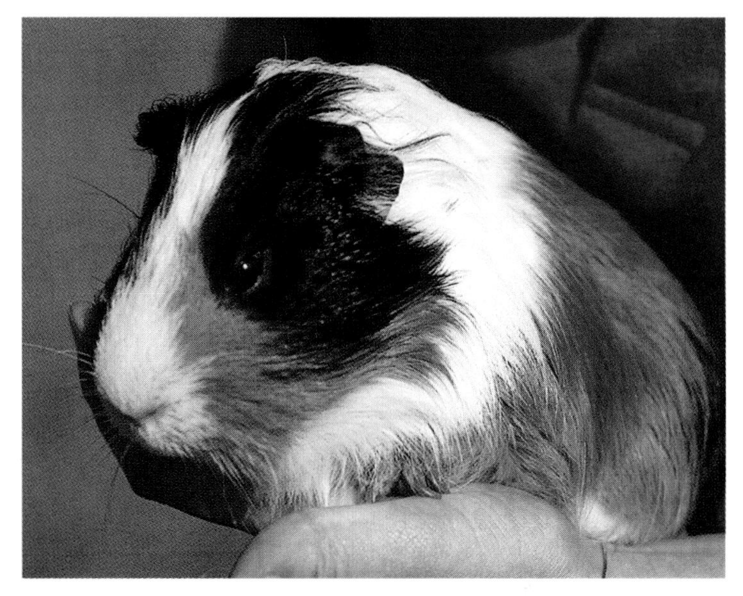

The proper way to hold a guinea pig is to use two hands and to cradle him close to your body. Falling, even from a low height, can seriously injure or kill your pet.

If you hold your guinea pig in your lap to tickle him behind the ears, you might want to place a towel or baby changing pad over your lap. A guinea pig will not wait to urinate until he is back in his cage. If your pet is feeling especially pleased while being petted, he might chatter his teeth together.

It is important that your guinea pig gets enough of the essential vitamins necessary to his good health in his daily diet. Some pelleted foods are fortified with long-lasting vitamin C to ensure your guinea pig gets enough of this important vitamin, as well as other fundamental nutrients. Photo courtesy of Kaytee Products, Inc.

CHOOSING

The best age to buy a guinea pig is when he is six to eight weeks old or about six inches long. Choose a lively guinea pig that does not cower and hide in a corner. One that is curious and interested in your hand, even if he is somewhat shy, will be a good pet. Short-haired guinea pigs are easier to care for than the long-haired breeds. The long-haired varieties need to be brushed each day and, because their hair grows continuously, it must be trimmed every few weeks. Abyssinian guinea pigs (those that have rosettes in their coats) also need regular grooming with a soft brush such as a toothbrush.

HOUSING AND ACCESSORIES

Since guinea pigs do not climb, they need roomy wire cages with lots of floor space. A single guinea pig should have a cage that measures at least two square feet. Add another square foot for each additional guinea pig housed in the same cage. A pair of guinea pigs can also be housed in a 20-gallon aquarium. Although guinea pigs cannot jump, their aquarium should be covered with a wire screen to protect them from other animals. Because aquariums have reduced air flow, you must be vigilant about keeping such a cage clean.

Use shavings as bedding in your guinea pig's cage. Loose hay is good nesting material, and guinea pigs enjoy nibbling and burrowing through it. Wrap a cloth or plastic seed guard around the base of a wire cage to prevent your guinea pig from kicking out bedding and making a mess. Guinea pigs need cages with solid floors. Wire floors can make their feet sore, and their feet can sometimes get caught and twisted in the wire. If you do use a wire cage, place a layer of bedding over the wire bottom of the cage to make a protective, comfortable carpet for your guinea pig's feet.

Provide a cozy nest box in which your guinea pig can sleep. Unlike other small furry pets, guinea pigs do not play with toys, but they will gnaw on wooden chew sticks. They also enjoy clambering up onto their nest box or a wooden shelf.

FEEDING

Guinea pigs are herbivorous. Feed them commercial alfalfa pellets made specifically for guinea pigs. Like people, guinea pigs must derive vitamin C from their food, which is why it is important to feed them guinea pig food. Although rabbit pellets might look the same as guinea pig pellets, they do not contain vitamin C. A guinea pig that is fed rabbit pellets will become sick and develop scurvy.

Small pieces of fresh vegetables and fruits are good treats for your guinea pig. He will also enjoy a handful of grass, clover, or dandelion leaves, but be careful to collect wild food from places that have not been sprayed with insecticides, weed killers, or fertilizers. Wash these treats thoroughly before giving them to your guinea pig.

Guinea pigs nibble throughout the day, so be

Guinea pigs should be housed in a roomy cage, and they are quite happy to have companions.

sure yours always have food. They are creatures of habit and routine, so feed them at the same time each day. Provide a gnawing block and a salt and mineral lick for them as well. Give your guinea pig fresh water in a water bottle.

Sometimes a guinea pig can become overweight. If your pet feels soft with a flabby potbelly, he might need a food with fewer calories, such as one based on timothy hay rather than alfalfa.

SPECIAL NEEDS

If you have a backyard, make a portable grazing run for your guinea pig to use during warm weather. The run can be a wooden-framed cage covered with wire mesh. About one-third of the run should be covered to protect him from the weather and to give him a place to retreat if frightened.

Move the run from place to place so that he has fresh grass every day. Be sure the grass is not treated with fertilizer, herbicides, or pesticides. You will be surprised to see your normally placid pet bound with abandon in the grass.

BREEDING

Because of their long gestation period (63 to 70 days), guinea pigs do not breed as prolifically as other rodents. Their first breeding can occur at two months. Baby guinea pigs are born with fur and with their eyes open. They can run around right after birth. They begin to eat solid food by their second day, and they are weaned after three weeks. A litter usually contains two to four guinea pigs.

Your guinea pig can snack on nutritious, fortified, fun-to-eat treat sticks that are available at your local pet shop in a variety of flavors. Photo courtesy of Kaytee Products, Inc.

Baby guinea pigs are born with fur and open eyes and mature rapidly. These guinea pigs are just one day old, but they are almost ready to eat solid food.

Hamsters

In 1930, an Israeli scientist on an expedition to Syria discovered an underground nest containing a family of golden hamsters. He brought the mother and her seven youngsters back to Hebrew University. Only three of the original group survived, one male and two females. It is believed that these three hamsters are the ancestors of most pet hamsters.

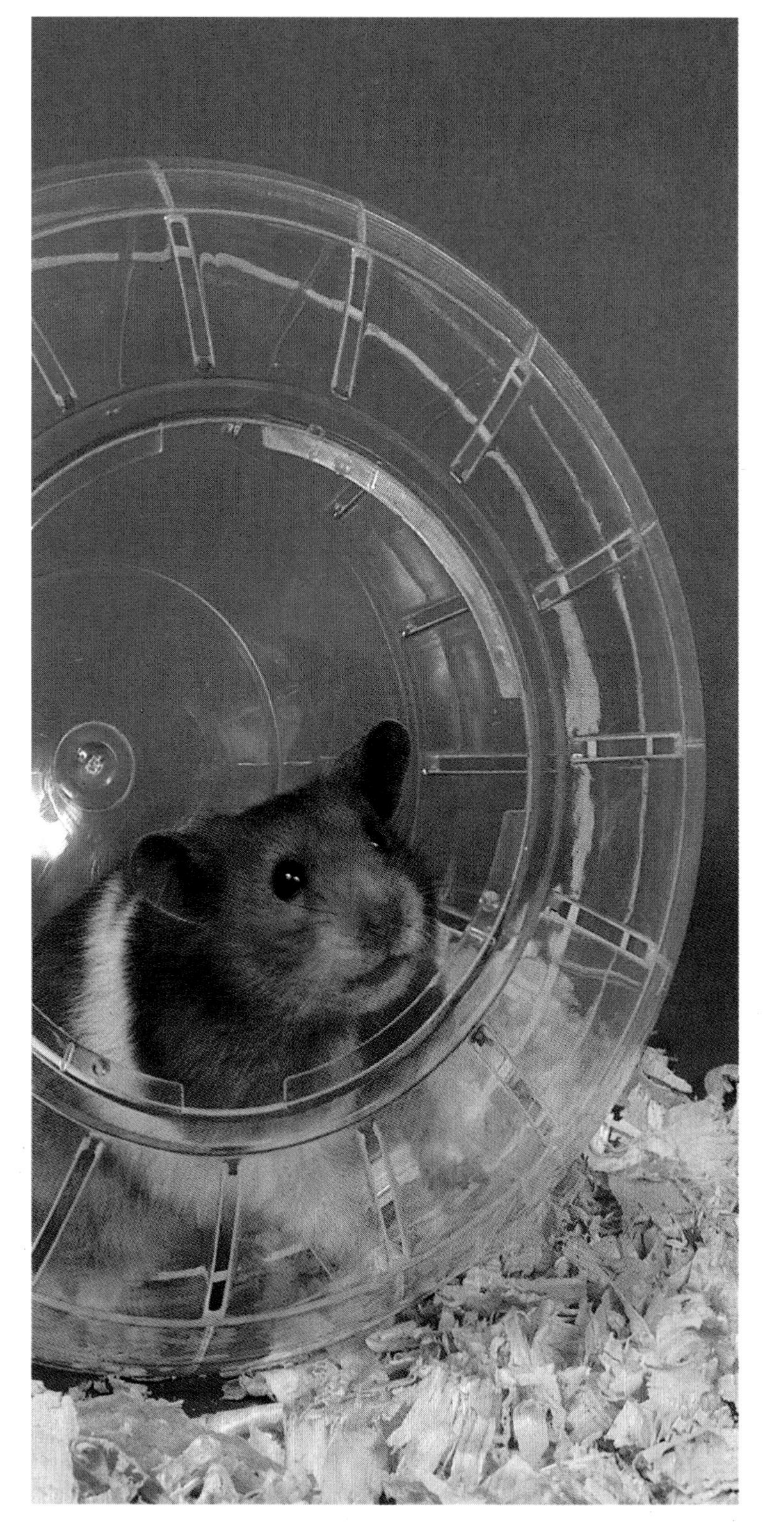

An exercise ball is a good way to let your hamster safely explore your home. Make sure to keep him away from stairs, because he might accidentally roll down them while he's playing in his ball.

DESCRIPTION

Hamsters are cute little animals with short legs and a small tail. They measure about six inches in length. Because they have poor vision, hamsters rely on their ears, nose, and whiskers to investigate their surroundings. Their keen sense of smell helps them find food and even helps them to recognize their owner. Secretions from skin glands located on their hips are used to mark their territory and attract a mate. Hamsters have

Hamsters have large cheek pouches that extend down over their shoulders. They use their pouches to store food to carry back to their nests. Hoarding food helps them survive in the wild when food is scarce.

This long-haired, or Teddy Bear, variety of hamster is just one of more than 30 available color patterns and coat types.

These Russian Dwarf hamsters—one albino, the other the standard agouti color—are smaller and more active than the golden hamster. Dwarf hamsters are becoming very popular as pets.

large cheek pouches that extend down over their shoulders. They use their pouches to carry food back to their nest to store. In the wild, the habit of hoarding food helps hamsters survive when food is scarce.

VARIETIES

Because the golden hamster was first found in Syria, it is also known as the Syrian hamster. More than 30 varieties of the golden hamster have been developed. Some of the most popular colors are cream, fawn, silver blue, and piebalds. At least three coat types have been developed: satin (a striking, glossy coat), long-haired, and rex (a rough curly coat with the long guard hairs short or absent). In recent years, two species of dwarf hamsters have become available as pets. They are smaller than the golden hamster, more active and entertaining, and more bold and curious. Be careful when choosing a pet dwarf hamster. Some strains are temperamental and ornery.

Never house more than one hamster in a cage. They are territorial animals and will sometimes fight to the death if forced to share their living space.

FEMALE AND MALE

Female hamsters are larger than male hamsters. Females can be distinguished from males by their visible teats and blunt hindquarters. Males have a visible scrotum, sloping hindquarters, and more obvious skin glands on their hips. Some people think male hamsters are easier to tame than females, but it depends on the individual animal.

HOW MANY?

Only one hamster should be kept in a cage. Your pet will not get lonely, because hamsters are not social animals. If housed together, hamsters will fight, often causing the death of one combatant.

AS PETS

Hamsters are popular pets because they are quiet, inexpensive, and easy to care for. If tamed and handled correctly, they will be friendly. Many hamsters do not like to be held and are prone to bite if irritated. It is important, therefore, to start off right with your hamster. Do not try to hold him right away. Instead, give him a few days to get settled into his new home. Be gentle and patient when taming him, because it will take several weeks to gain his trust. Begin by lightly tapping on his cage and using his name to call him out of his nest. Talk gently and offer him a tasty treat from your hand. After a few days, your hamster will be more confident, and you can pet him in his cage or when he crawls on your hand. Eventually, you will be able to pick him up and cuddle him.

Hamsters sleep curled in a ball with their head tucked between their legs. Do not try to pick up or disturb your hamster when he is asleep. They can be crabby (just as you might be) if startled or awakened from a deep sleep. Even a tame hamster is likely to bite under these circumstances. Wait to play with your pet until late afternoon or early evening, when he is already awake.

Hamsters are territorial and do not like their nest and food hoarding area disturbed. Some hamsters will bite if you intrude in this area. An annoyed hamster will roll on his back, lay back his ears, bare his teeth, and even growl.

Hamsters are most active at night. When they are awake, hamsters are very busy. They constantly check and add to their store of food.

Every hamster needs an exercise wheel. Hamsters may travel on their wheels up to five miles each night.

As with all small pets, it's best to use two hands when holding your hamster.

Your hamster will stuff food into his cheek pouches, scurry back to his nest, and empty the pouches by pushing against his neck with his front paws. (Be sure to check on his food hoard during your weekly cleaning and remove any food that is spoiled.) Making and remaking their nest is also a favorite activity.

Hamsters' acrobatic antics are entertaining to watch. In wire cages, hamsters dangle and climb from the top of the cage using only their two front paws. Running on their exercise wheel occupies them for hours.

Your active hamster needs an exercise wheel. During the night, he may travel up to five miles on his wheel. Also, let your hamster out of his cage to explore, but play with him on the floor. Although small in size, hamsters are bold, fearless, and curious. Hamsters are not afraid of heights and can easily fall out of your hands or off a table or bed and get hurt. Carefully supervise your hamster when he crawls around, so that he cannot escape.

LIFE SPAN

About 2 years

HANDLING

Pick up your hamster by slipping one hand under his belly and quickly cupping your other hand over his back and in front of his face. Always hold your hamster with both hands. Hamsters are wiggly and can suddenly jump out of your hands, especially if they are surprised by sudden movements or a loud noise. Hold your hamster close to your body for extra security.

CHOOSING

A young hamster, about six to eight weeks old (or about four inches long) is easier to tame than an older one. Try to buy your hamster in the early evening or morning when he is more likely to be awake and active. A hamster that is curious and sniffs your hand or lets you pet his side is a good choice.

HOUSING AND ACCESSORIES

An array of cages are sold for hamsters—from wire models to colorful plastic modular cages that can be continually expanded. Keep your hamster in a cage that measures at least 18 in. long x 12 in. wide x 10 in. high. Hamster cages must be escape-proof, with a strong door latch. Some hamsters will chew their way out of molded plastic cages. Line the bottom of your hamster's cage with shavings. Provide commercial bedding material or hay for your hamster to build his nest.

Many toys have been designed for energetic hamsters. Your hamster will enjoy crawling through colorful plastic tubes, running on exercise wheels, and scampering up and down ladders. Give your hamster a place to sleep, such as a ceramic shoe or a cardboard home designed to be chewed.

Hamsters and gerbils are sociable animals and will enjoy interacting with you—especially for a treat! Favorite treats will be those that are tasty, nutritious, and chewy. Photo courtesy of Eight in One Pet Products.

Many fancy toys and accessories are available for your small pet at the local pet store. A nest box like this one, whether homemade or store-bought, will make your hamster feel snug and secure.

Use a plastic roll-about ball to let your hamster safely explore a room.

FEEDING

Hamsters are easy to feed. A variety of nutritionally complete, prepared hamster mixes are available from your local pet store. Always be sure your pet has food. Keep in mind that your hamster will empty his food dish and store the tastier tidbits in a cage corner under the bedding. Feed him small pieces of fresh vegetables and fruits as treats, but give him only as much as he can eat in a few minutes and remove any excess. Fresh foods that are stored in your hamster's hoard could spoil and cause him to become ill. Provide fresh water in a water bottle.

SPECIAL NEEDS

Hamsters are persistent escape artists. If your hamster disappears from his cage or when you let him out to play, calmly search the house for him. A noisy, frantic search could frighten your hamster and cause him to hide. If you cannot find your pet, place his cage on the floor next to a wall in the room from which he escaped. Leave the cage door open with his favorite treats inside and a small trail of shavings leading to the door. Your hamster will probably return to his cage by the next day.

BREEDING

The breeding cycle of hamsters is among the fastest of all mammals. They can breed at 7 weeks and have a 16-day gestation period. Litters range in size from 1 to 16 hamsters, with an average of 6 to 8. Young hamster pups are born pink and hairless but develop rapidly. By the end of the second week, they can eat solid food, and they are weaned after 21 to 28 days.

Fancy Mice

Fancy mice are a domesticated form of the house mouse. The wild house mouse is a destructive pest that is found throughout the world and lives in close association with people and their stored food. The house mouse has been selectively bred in captivity for more than a century. It was first domesticated as a small laboratory animal for use in scientific research. Fancy mice have been kept as pets almost as long as they have been used in laboratories.

DESCRIPTION

Mice are slim animals with wide hindquarters. Full-grown mice are small and measure between four and six inches in body length. Mice have a slender pink tail that is almost as long as their body. Their tails are prehensile and help them to climb. Compared with rats, mice have larger ears and their noses are more pointed. Long whiskers and special sensory hairs located all over their bodies help them

Mice have larger ears than rats and their noses are more pointed. They are available in more than 50 different varieties.

Fancy mice are a domesticated form of the wild house mouse, a destructive pest that is found throughout the world.

Four coat types have been developed in the mouse. This one, a rex, has curly fur.

This lilac-and-tan female mouse's long tail is prehensile, meaning she uses it to help her climb.

detect their environment. Their bulging eyes give them a wide field of vision, but their ability to smell is their strongest sense.

VARIETIES

Decades of selective breeding have produced more than 50 color varieties of mice, and four coat types have been developed: satin, astrex, long-haired, and rex. Marked varieties include broken-marked mice, which have colored spots or patches distributed over a white background. Eye color is either black or red. Ear size and shape can also vary among the different varieties. Exotic species of mice, such as spiny mice, are not as easily tamed and are not a good beginner's pet.

FEMALE AND MALE

Male mice are called bucks, and females are called does. Males use urine to mark their territory and have a very strong "mousy" smell. Because they fight as adults, male mice should not be kept together. However, the risk of fighting is reduced if the males were littermates or the same age and already acquainted when young. Females can be housed with each other or with one male (if you want baby mice). Females tend to be more active and curious than males.

HOW MANY

A mouse can be kept on his own but will need your attention if you are his only playmate. Mice are social by nature and live most happily in pairs (two females or a mixed pair) or larger groups (one male and a group of females). A new mouse added to an existing cage of mice will be attacked. Introduce the new mouse by first placing it in a separate cage adjacent to the established cage of mice for about one week. Then switch the mice to each other's cages, so they become familiar with one another's scents before moving them into the same cage. Even when a familiar mouse is removed from the cage (for example, to take it to the vet), it must be gradually reintroduced because it might be attacked when reunited with its cagemates.

AS PETS

Mice are easy pets to keep because they do not need any specialized care. Their small size makes them easy to hold and play with. Mice are timid, gentle animals that must be treated and handled kindly. These tiny animals like to hide and ride in their owner's pockets. Some mice also enjoy riding on their owner's shoulder. Mice are fairly intelligent and can be trained to do simple things.

Mice are awake and active for short periods during both the day and night. When awake, they are lively and entertaining to watch as they scamper and frolic about their cage. Mice like toys, and providing new and interesting ones is a challenge. They can spend hours climbing up and down a thick parrot rope dangling from the roof of their cage, tunneling through cardboard tubes, and running on their exercise wheel. They are inquisitive animals and will escape if there is any weakness in their cage.

Young mice become tame fairly quickly, especially if you use food treats to encourage them to approach you. Let your mouse get to know you by placing your hand inside his cage and

Many mice, such as this black Dutch female, enjoy riding in their owners' pockets.

Be it ever so humble, your mouse needs a house. An aquarium with a wire mesh top is a good choice. Here, a cardboard box, egg carton, and two toilet paper rolls create chewable furniture, and the addition of a swing and exercise wheel (solid-frame is preferable) makes this an ideal living environment for a little pet.

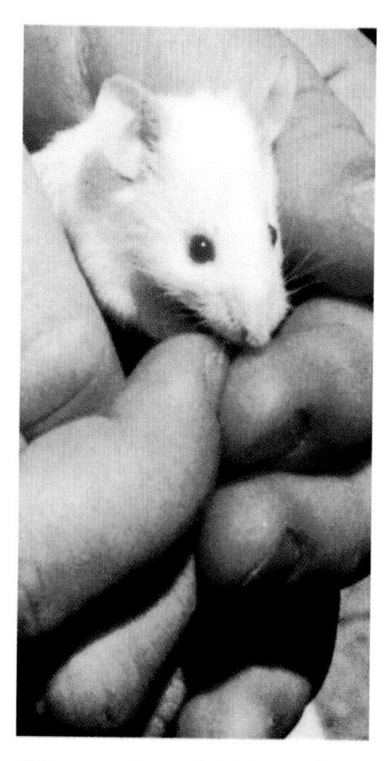

Mice are quick and skittish and must be held securely—but never squeezed—in two hands.

allowing him to sniff and crawl on your hand. Do this for several days before you try to pick him up. Mice like to be let out of their cage to play and explore, but be sure to watch them carefully, because they can quickly disappear.

A mouse's cage needs to be cleaned frequently to prevent odor, usually at least twice a week. The more animals kept in a cage, the more often you will have to clean their cage. If you have male mice, you may want to clean their cage as often as every day. Mice do not always establish a bathroom area in their cage, but defecate and urinate anywhere, even in their food dish (although some do use the cage corners more often). A cage with a pull-out pan can make cage cleaning easier. Odor control products sold in pet stores will help reduce any smell the mice produce.

LIFE SPAN

About 2 years

HANDLING

Pick up your mouse in one hand, but use two hands to hold him. Many mice do not stay still when they are held. They continually run from one hand to the next. Block your mouse's movements and potential jumps by placing one hand in front of his face. Gently hold your pet near the base of his tail for added security. (Never hold a mouse by the end of his tail.) Do not squeeze your mouse or he will become frightened and panic. Although mice bite infrequently, they will bite if they are scared. Once tame, a mouse will feel secure when held and will not try to escape. Then you will not need to hold your pet by his tail.

CHOOSING

Most mice in pet stores are sold as "feeders," meaning snake food. Some of these mice are not very good specimens. Let the store personnel know you are buying a pet mouse so they will show you their best stock. Choose a mouse that is relatively calm and not frantic and jumpy when held. Do not buy a mouse that nips. A baby mouse can be bought when he is about four weeks old (or about one to two inches in body length). Young mice tame more quickly than older ones and make better pets.

HOUSING AND ACCESSORIES

Mice are active animals that like to climb, jump, and run. They do best in a roomy cage that measures at least 15 in. long x 10 in. wide x 10 in. high. Mice can be housed in either wire cages or ten-gallon glass aquariums. If you use a wire cage, make certain that the space between the wires is not larger than a quarter of an inch, or your mouse will be able to squeeze out of the cage. Mice enjoy climbing and exploring a wire cage that has several stories.

Mice can jump surprisingly high, so be sure to cover an aquarium with a wire screen that clips to the top. Your mice might surprise you by climbing up the water bottle hanging inside their aquarium and walking upside down on the wire screen. A ten-gallon aquarium can comfortably house a small group of mice (e.g., one male and three females). Because mice do not burrow, use a shallow layer of shavings in their cage.

Give your mice a nest box to sleep in. They will make a soft bed out of unscented tissue paper, commercial nesting material, or an old sock. Toys are important for mice. Provide toys designed for hamsters and wood toys sold for birds. An exercise wheel, paper towel tubes, wicker nests, fruit tree branches, ladders, hanging swings, and nuts in a shell will give your pet hours of entertainment. Some of your mouse's toys will pick up a "mousy" smell and will need to be replaced often, and the mouse might shred or gnaw others.

FEEDING

Like rats, mice are omnivorous, which means they eat fruits and vegetables, grains, seeds, nuts, and meat. A hamster or gerbil mix is a good basic diet for your mice. Also add different types of bird seed to the mix, such as parakeet, finch, and parrot food. Feed them only small amounts of fresh foods, such as carrots and apples. Remove whatever is not eaten within 10 to 15 minutes. Fresh food can quickly spoil and make your mice sick. Mice eat throughout the day and should always have food available. Do not be fooled into thinking the food dish is full by the empty seed chaff. Dump the chaff and refill the bowl with new food. Mice also like honey seed treat sticks that are sold for birds. These treats are a good way to ensure they always have food available. Mice also enjoy treats, such as hard dog biscuits or an occasional small mealworm. Give them fresh water in a water bottle.

SPECIAL NEEDS

Tumors can sometimes be a problem in mice older than one year. Obesity can also be a problem in older mice. Do not feed your mice too many fatty foods such as sunflower seeds.

BREEDING

Mice are prolific breeders beginning as early as 10 to 12 weeks of age. Pregnant females become huge as they near their delivery date and should not be handled. After a 20-day gestation period, baby mice are born pink and helpless but start moving around the cage at two weeks of age. A group of females will often share the task of nursing each other's offspring. A typical litter averages nine mice. If your family of mice live in a wire cage, be sure the wire mesh is not so large that the babies can fall through the mesh. Baby mice are weaned between 21 and 28 days.

Mice love to eat, and their omnivorous diet makes them fun to feed. Fruits, vegetables, grains, seeds, nuts, and meat are all acceptable mouse foods.

Rabbits

Rabbits are not rodents. They are classified in the order Lagomorpha, because they have six incisor (front) teeth (two tiny teeth are located behind their upper incisors), as opposed to rodents, which only have four incisors. About 25 species of rabbit are found in the world, but only one species (*Oryctolagus cuniculus*), originally from the Iberian Peninsula, has been domesticated. This species of rabbit was first used as a source of food during the Middle Ages. Since then, domesticated rabbits have been introduced by people, accidentally and intentionally, to most parts of the world. People began breeding the specialized varieties of rabbit found today more than 100 years ago.

People love rabbits for their long ears, short fluffy tails, and very soft fur. They are responsive and affectionate and make great indoor pets.

DESCRIPTION

Rabbits have long hind legs, short fluffy tails, and long erect ears (except for lop-eared rabbits, which have ears that hang down). Unlike most animals, rabbits do not walk, they hop. They also stand on their hind legs to look around. Their large ears help to capture and amplify sound, and their large eyes placed on the sides of their head help them see behind them almost as well as they can see in front. Rabbits are herbivorous animals and are preyed on in the wild by many types of animals. Unlike many of the other small furry animals, rabbits do not hold food in their front paws, but eat with all four feet on the ground.

Dwarf rabbits make particularly good pets for children, because they are smaller and easier to handle.

VARIETIES

Rabbits come in a wide range of colors and sizes and a variety of coat types. More

Lop rabbits have long ears that hang down instead of standing up straight.

These two Holland Lops will keep each other company if their owner is not able to give them enough attention every day.

than 40 breeds of pedigreed rabbit are recognized. The smallest breed, the Netherland dwarf, weighs only about two pounds and is a popular pet. The largest breed, the Flemish giant, weighs more than 14 pounds and is used mainly for meat and fur, although they make friendly pets. Some of the larger breeds can be difficult to handle and need a lot of room. The long-haired Angora is not a good choice for a first-time owner, because grooming is a time-consuming daily activity. Some rabbits are mixed breeds and, just like with mixed-breed dogs, you will not know for sure how large they will grow.

FEMALE AND MALE

Female rabbits are called does and males are called bucks. Does are slightly larger than bucks. Some people think males are calmer than females, but this is a matter of opinion. Be aware that unneutered males often spray urine. Once rabbits reach sexual maturity, their personality can change. A veterinarian can spay or neuter your pet rabbit. These procedures will prevent unwanted pregnancies and reduce aggression and territorial marking.

Long-haired breeds of rabbit like this Rhinelander are not a good choice for the first-time owner, because they require an enormous amount of grooming.

HOW MANY?

Rabbits are social animals and need daily attention. If you will not be able to give your rabbit enough attention, buy two young rabbits. You can keep two neutered males, a neutered male and a female, or two females together. (Of course, an unneutered male and female kept together will produce offspring.) If you buy two rabbits, be aware that in a pair, one rabbit will dominate the other and they may fight.

AS PETS

Rabbits are hardy, easy to care for, cute, and friendly. They are responsive, affectionate pets that can learn their names and, in some cases, simple commands. Their soft fur and large eyes make it hard to resist them. Tame rabbits like to interact with their owners, and some enjoy being petted, but most rabbits prefer not to be held and will not sit on your lap for long before demanding to be put down.

Many rabbits like to be petted, but most don't like to be held. This very tame Netherland Dwarf rabbit is happier sitting next to his owner for petting instead of on her lap.

When your rabbit wants to play, he will butt into you or nip at your leg and run away. Rabbits are good housepets, and many can be litter box trained. They take naps throughout the day and are most active in the early morning and evening.

It will take a few weeks for you to tame your rabbit. Talk to him quietly and move slowly in his presence. Quick, jerky movements will scare him. The more attention you give your rabbit, the more tame and friendly he will be.

Although a rabbit does not demand as much attention as a dog, if you neglect your rabbit, he can become skittish, easily frightened, and difficult to handle and control. Therefore, choose a rabbit as a pet only if you can devote time to interact with him each day. They are a good alternative for an apartment dweller who cannot own a cat or dog.

Ideally, rabbits should be allowed out of their cage for exercise at least once a day. Sometimes, your rabbit might dash around the room, happily leaping and twirling like a dancer. Watch him closely, because some rabbits chew furniture and electrical cords, dig up carpets, and try to escape. Outside, use a wire grazing run, with a wire floor (so he cannot dig out) and a sheltered area to let your pet exercise and graze. Some rabbits can be supervised on a harness and leash, but they cannot be trained to walk on a leash like a dog. Think of this method instead as a safe way of allowing your pet to explore as you follow along.

It is best not to use a harness until your rabbit is

full-grown, at around seven months. The harness must fit properly so the rabbit cannot get loose. Most rabbits need to get used to a harness and leash and must learn to comfortably walk in one without struggling or darting away. Train your pet to accept the harness and leash indoors before going outside. Patience and short training sessions are important. Be careful about potential outdoor hazards such as hot pavement, temperature extremes, and other animals such as dogs and cats. Never leave your rabbit unattended when he is in his harness.

Your small pet will enjoy sampling a variety of nutritious treats in tasty flavors like corn, alfalfa, and carrot. Look for products that are made with real vegetables and enriched with vitamins and minerals. Photo courtesy of Vitakraft Pet Products Company, Inc.

Your rabbit can learn to explore the outdoors on a leash with a little patience and training.

Because they are large animals and drink a lot of water, rabbits produce a lot of urine and droppings. Rabbits usually choose one corner of their cage for a bathroom area, and this area should be cleaned once a day. Some rabbits will use a litter box if it is placed in their cage away from their food area.

LIFE SPAN

6 to 10 years

HANDLING

It is always best to use two hands to pick up and hold your rabbit, regardless of his size. To pick up your rabbit, use one hand to grab the loose skin at the base of his neck and use your other hand to lift and support his rear end. Hold your rabbit in your arms next to your body. With smaller, tame rabbits, scoop your hand underneath their body to lift them, rather than lifting them by the scruff of the neck. If you hold your rabbit gently, he will not mind

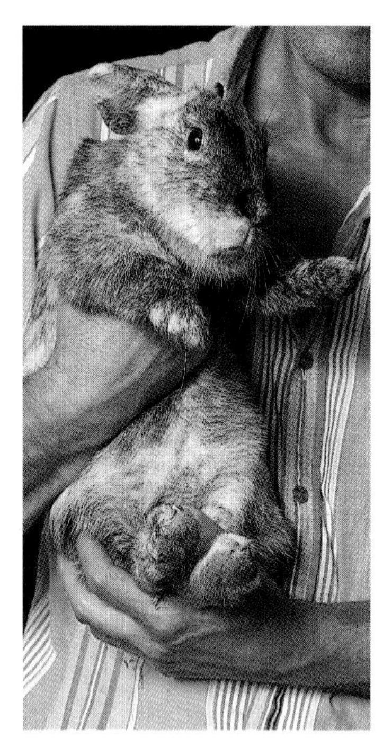

To pick up your rabbit, scoop him up with one hand underneath his body as you support his hind legs with the other hand. Hold him gently, close to your body for security.

being picked up and will usually stay calm in your arms for a short time. Be careful when handling your rabbit. If frightened, he will kick with his hind legs to get away and may inflict painful scratches. If you drop your rabbit, he could be seriously injured.

CHOOSING

Choose a young rabbit—at least eight weeks old—to be your pet. The size of a young rabbit will vary, depending on the breed. A lively, inquisitive rabbit that sniffs your hand is a good choice. He should feel plump and be somewhat relaxed when held.

Different breeds of rabbit were developed for different purposes, such as for meat, fur, looks, or temperament. Each breed varies in personality and temperament. Do some research and talk to people who know about rabbits to help you select a rabbit that is right for you.

HOUSING AND ACCESSORIES

Rabbits should be housed in a roomy wire cage of at least three square feet. The actual cage size depends on the adult size of your rabbit. Larger rabbits, such as French lops, will need a larger cage. In general, the bigger the cage the better, although finding a place in your house to keep a large cage can sometimes be a problem. The cage should provide plenty of floor space and should be tall enough for the rabbit to comfortably stand up on his hind feet. Enough space for a sleeping compartment is also important. Outside hutches are a housing option in some of the warmer parts of the country.

Shavings and a layer of straw for nibbling make good

These five little Dutch Dwarfs are adorable, but they are too young to go to new homes yet. Eight weeks old is the ideal age for your new bunny.

It's important for small mammals to get variety in their diets. A tasty blend of navy, pinto, and red kidney beans with corn, sunflower seeds, and hearty greens will satisfy their nutritional needs and their taste buds! Photo courtesy of Eight in One Pet Products.

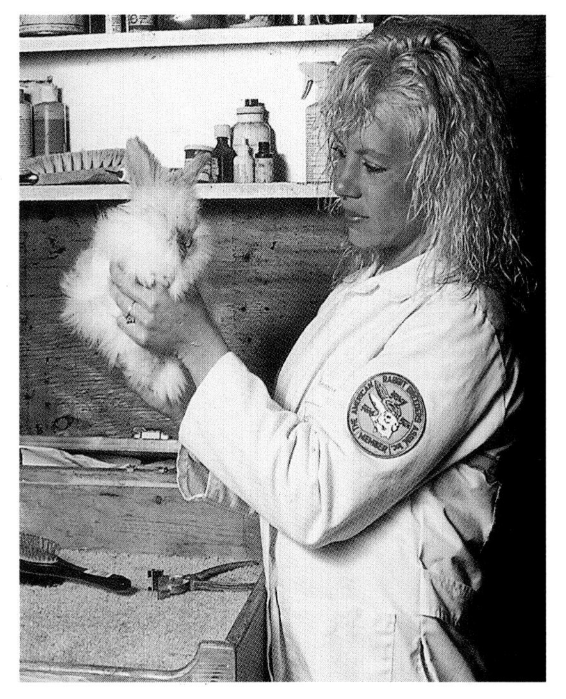

If you wish to keep long-haired rabbits, you may want to use a professional groomer to keep their coats in good condition.

bedding for your rabbit. Provide your pet with a nest box. If the cage is large enough, a corner litter box can be left in it for your rabbit to use.

FEEDING

Rabbits are easy to feed. Commercial rabbit pellets, which are made of alfalfa, cereal grains, and minerals and vitamins, are inexpensive and contain a balanced diet for your pet. Loose hay, such as timothy or alfalfa, should make up at least half of your pet's diet. Rabbits enjoy treats of fresh cabbage, lettuce, carrots, dandelion, clover, and grasses. Add fresh greens to your rabbit's diet gradually, and feed him only as much as he will eat in a half-hour. To avoid digestive upset, don't feed fresh greens to a rabbit until he is at least six months old. Because rabbits graze throughout the day, they should always have loose hay available. Feed your rabbit carefully measured amounts of rabbit pellets, because they are high in calories and can lead to obesity in some overfed rabbits. Rabbits drink a lot of water, so be sure their water bottle is always full, especially on a hot day.

SPECIAL NEEDS

Rabbits are clean animals and bathe themselves as often as cats do. Like cats, rabbits can get furballs and become constipated. They also molt several times a year and can shed on your clothes. To prevent the furball and shedding problems, gently groom your rabbit using a rubber shedding brush. Fleas can be transmitted to your rabbit from other household pets, such as a dog or cat. Use a flea comb to remove the fleas. Cat flea products are usually safe to use on rabbits, but check with your veterinarian to be sure.

BREEDING

The age of a rabbit's first breeding depends on the breed but is generally between five and nine months. A pregnant doe will pull out fur from her chest and stomach to make a nest for her babies. After 28 to 31 days, baby rabbits are born with no hair and with their eyes closed. The litter size varies between 1 and 12 bunnies (or kits); 4 to 6 is the average litter size. The bunnies need to stay with their mother for eight weeks, until they are weaned.

Rats

There are hundreds of different species of rat found all over the world. The most notorious species are the destructive brown and black rats, which have lived with people for centuries. It is believed that the brown rat was first domesticated in the early 1800s for use in ratting contests with dogs. By the late 18th century, rats were being used for scientific studies. From the laboratory, rats found their way into homes as pets.

DESCRIPTION

Rats are slender animals that measure about 20 inches in length, including their long, scaly tails. Many people do not like the appearance of a rat's tail, but it serves several useful functions. It helps

Rats make surprisingly good pets. They are friendly, affectionate, and very intelligent.

The long, scaly tail of the rat helps him balance when he climbs. A full-grown rat measures about 20 inches in length, including his tail.

them balance when climbing, and the scales can ruffle backward and give the rat a good grip. Rats lack sweat glands, but they use their tails as thermoregulating devices. When a rat is cold, the blood vessels in his tail constrict to conserve heat. When he is hot, the same vessels radiate excess heat.

Rats have poor vision and can see well only when an object is close to their face. Their night vision is better, however. At night, they can see up to 30 feet away. The whiskers on their face and special sensory hairs on their body help them sense their environment. An acute sense of hearing allows them to perceive shrill notes that are too high for people to hear.

Rats have great night vision and very sharp hearing, which makes them well suited to their nocturnal existence.

VARIETIES

Rats come in a variety of fancy colors and markings. The most common colors include albino, black, champagne, creme, lilac, and agouti. The most common marked variety is the hooded rat, which has a colored hood that covers his head and shoulders and continues in a saddle down his back to the tail. Depending on their coat color, their eyes are either black or red. Rats come in three different coat types: smooth, curly-coated rex, and hairless.

FEMALE AND MALE

Female rats are called does and male rats are called bucks. Female rats are smaller and sleeker than male rats and tend to be more active. Male rats are more likely to sit happily in your lap while you scratch them behind their ears. Both sexes make excellent pets, but males are more likely to mark their territory with urine.

HOW MANY?

Rats are social animals and enjoy each other's company. A pair of rats will groom each other and play-wrestle. However, it is not necessary to keep rats together. A single rat might be more responsive and friendly, because you are his only playmate. Rats of either sex can be kept together, if purchased at the same time, although one rat will dominate the other.

AS PETS

Just as dogs differ from wolves, domestic rats are

different from their wild relatives. Much to many people's surprise, rats make excellent, loving pets. They are gentle, friendly, affectionate, and curious pets that thrive on human companionship and look forward to interacting with their owners. In the evening, your rat will greet you at his cage door, waiting to come out and play. Let him ride on your shoulder, carry him in your shirt pocket, or tuck him in your sleeve.

Because rats are not timid and rarely bite, they make excellent classroom pets. Like kittens, rats are playful animals and enjoy chasing and tackling a piece of paper tied to a string. If exploring a room, they will steal papers and other objects to take to their secret hiding places.

Rats have good memories and are extremely intelligent. Many scientists believe that rats are as smart as dogs. Your rat will learn his name and can be trained to come to you when called. You can even train your rat to perform clever tricks, such as navigating through a maze to reach a food reward.

Rats are nocturnal and, therefore, are most active in the evening. Unlike small animals such as hamsters, most rats will not use an exercise wheel. They prefer to be taken out of their cage to play with you and explore a room. Rats are naturally fastidiously clean animals and groom themselves throughout the day.

LIFE SPAN

3 years

HANDLING

Tame rats are docile and will not struggle or jump out of your hands. They are agile animals and can safely ride on your shoulder. To pick up your pet, scoop your hand underneath its belly and let it rest in both hands. Hold your pet next to your body for extra protection.

CHOOSING

Choose a young rat—four to eight weeks of age, or about four inches in body length. A bold, curious rat that investigates your hand when you put it into the cage is a good choice. Rats will usually dash away when you first put your hand in their cage but quickly return to further inspect your hand. Some rats are tame right away, relaxing when held in your hand, and will make a good pet. A frightened rat is tense, and you can feel his sharp nails in the palm of your hand. If he does not calm down after

Your pet rat will enjoy your company. He will ride on your shoulder, chase toys you provide, and happily accept treats.

You can train your rat to perform tricks, such as navigating through a maze to reach a food reward.

being held for a while, choose another one. Try to select a rat that does not sniffle when he breathes, because he might have a respiratory illness.

HOUSING AND ACCESSORIES

House your rat in a wire cage or ten-gallon aquarium. The cage should measure at least 20 in. long x 10 in. wide x 12 in. high. Use a larger cage for a pair of rats. If you use a wire cage, make sure the space between the bars is no larger than half an inch, or your rat might be able to squeeze out of the cage. Cover an aquarium with a wire screen that fastens with secure clips. Pine shavings are a good choice of bedding.

Rats need a nesting box for security and sleeping. Make a nest box from part of an empty milk carton or a cereal box, or buy one at a pet store.

This chocolate rat has everything he needs—food, water, comfortable bedding, and a roomy wire cage.

Place the box high in the cage, because rats like to climb and perch. Give the rat an old sock for nesting material. Your rat will play on wooden parrot toys, such as ladders, platforms, and swings.

FEEDING

Rats are omnivorous and, therefore, will eat fruits and vegetables, grains, seeds, nuts, and meat. Provide your rat with a nutritious diet by giving him a hamster or gerbil mix. Then add bird seed (e.g., fancy parrot mix), dry unsweetened cereals, bread, and crackers to this mix. Hard dog biscuits are also good for your rat and will help keep his teeth trim.

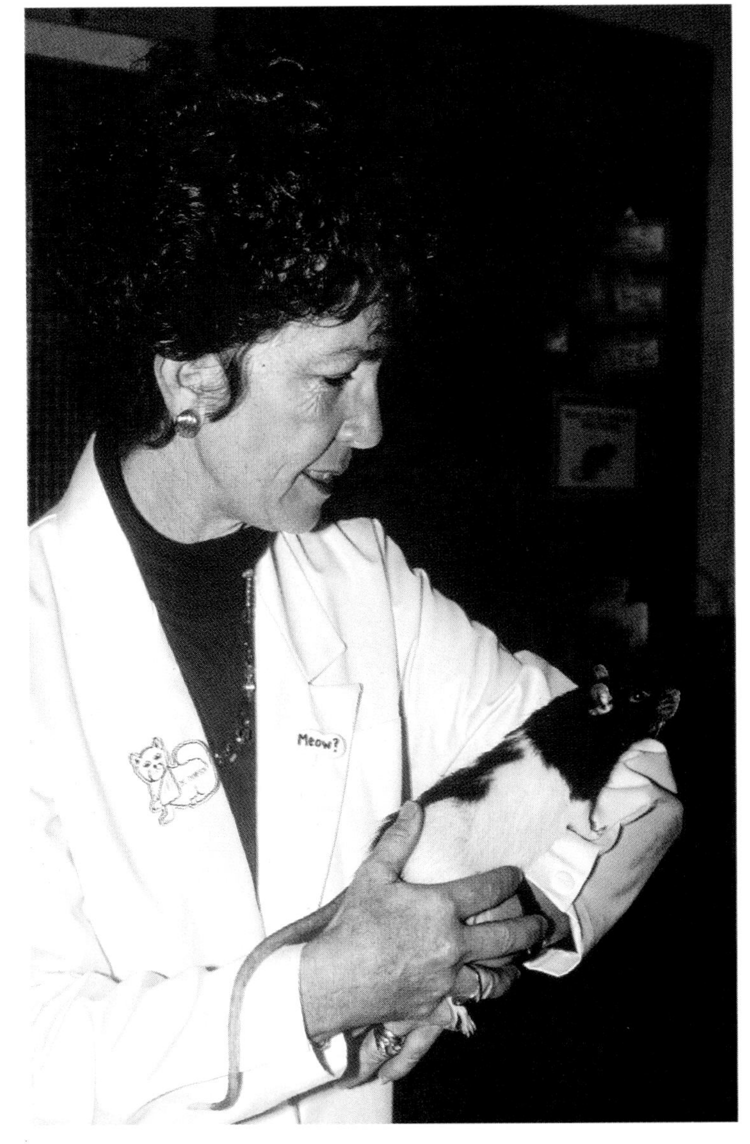

Many rats are afflicted with a common respiratory ailment causing sneezing, wheezing, and sniffling. A veterinarian can make your sick rat more comfortable with antibiotics.

A diet alternative is to feed your rat nutritionally balanced food pellets made especially for rats.

Give your rat treats of fruits, vegetables, and table scraps—for example, a small piece of potato with the skin on. Remember to remove any uneaten moist foods or feed only as much as your rat will eat in one sitting. Your rat should always have food available, but limit the amount of fatty items, such as sunflower seeds. It is best to feed your rat in the evening when he first wakes up. Provide fresh water in a water bottle.

SPECIAL NEEDS

It is sometimes difficult to find a pet rat that is not infected with the common ailment murine respiratory *Mycoplasma*. Symptoms of this disease are noisy breathing, including sneezing, wheezing, and sniffling. The disease is easily transmitted among rats. The onset is usually slow and progressive, although some infected rats do not show symptoms. Acute episodes can occur in young and old animals. It is not possible to cure an infected rat, but antibiotics prescribed by a veterinarian and dissolved in a rat's drinking water (use distilled water) will relieve his symptoms.

BREEDING

Rats are able to breed for the first time when they are between 50 and 60 days old. After a gestation period of 21 to 23 days, females give birth to a litter of 8 rats, on average. Baby rats are weaned between 25 and 32 days.

Grooming

Small animals are naturally clean. They spend up to 20 percent of their waking hours grooming themselves. Even those "dirty rats" spend a lot of time washing themselves—delicately cleaning each ear with their toes, then cleaning their toes, washing their front and backside, and even scrubbing their long tails. A small animal that cannot keep itself clean is probably sick and should have a veterinarian examine it.

Clean cages are one of the most important ways small animal owners can help their pets stay clean and well groomed. While grooming is usually synonymous with caring for hair, there are other aspects to grooming in small animal husbandry that are equally important.

SHEDDING

Rabbits and guinea pigs are the only small animals that shed any noticeable hair, especially when they molt. Some rabbits go through cycles of shedding every three months or so, and guinea pigs molt less often.

Long-haired breeds of rabbit and guinea pig, such as angoras and Peruvians, need daily brushing and regular trimming of their long coats. Short-haired varieties do not need to be groomed, but many animals enjoy being brushed with a soft brush or toothbrush. Other small animals, such as hamsters, gerbils, and mice, do not need to have their coats brushed. However, if they will hold still, you can brush these small pets with a toothbrush. Grooming sessions are a good time for you to notice whether your pet has a rough coat, dry

All small animals spend a good deal of time grooming themselves—washing their faces with their paws, combing their fur with their paws and teeth, and scrubbing their tails.

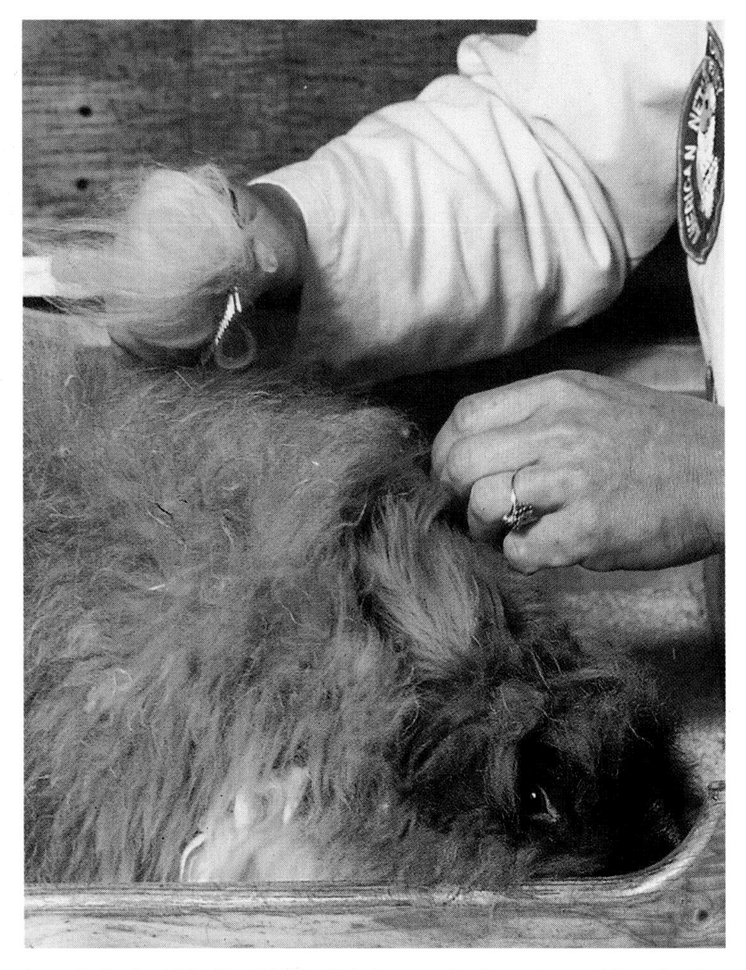

Long-haired rabbits like this English Angora shed great quantities of soft hair, which can be knitted into wonderful, warm sweaters. Guinea pigs, particularly the long-haired Peruvian variety, also shed. These animals need daily brushing and regular trimming.

skin, lumps, scabs, or evidence of external parasites, such as flea dirt.

Hairballs can present problems in rabbits and long-haired guinea pigs. Animals sometimes swallow a lot of hair when they groom themselves, especially when they are molting. Symptoms typically include lethargy, lack of appetite, and constipation. Depending on the species, surgery is sometimes necessary. Veterinarians sometimes recommend that cat hairball medicine be given to rabbits prophylactically—check with your rabbit's vet to see if this is all right. For rabbits, the addition of loose hay, which is high in fiber, can help prevent hairballs and other intestinal problems.

TEETH

Rodents and rabbits have chisel-like incisors in the front of their mouths. These teeth never stop growing, and in some species, they can grow up to five inches in a year. The incisors are worn down by the animal's gnawing and chewing on hard substances.

Pet stores sell a variety of wood chews to help small pets keep their teeth trim. In addition to keeping pets' teeth in shape, chew toys keep pets busy and active. Some types of chews are fruit-flavored and colorful. Other products serve a dual purpose: They are a nest box for the animal to sleep in but are meant to be chewed and destroyed over time.

The teeth of small animals sometimes need veterinary attention because of malocclusion. This condition occurs when an animal's incisor teeth do not meet properly, either because the teeth are overgrown or misaligned. The animal can die if the malocclusion prevents it from feeding. Malocclusion is sometimes called "slobbers," because symptoms include threads of saliva around the animal's mouth. Malocclusion can be inherited, dietary (for example, the animal does not regularly eat foods hard enough to wear down its teeth), or caused by an infection. An affected animal should be taken to a veterinarian, who will painlessly clip the animal's teeth.

NAILS

The nails of small animals grow continuously. Many pet owners complain that long, sharp nails can make handling their pets unpleasant at times. Besides being sharp on human skin, long nails present a hazard to a pet that is allowed to roam loose in the house. Long nails can get caught in carpeting, and an animal's unnoticed struggles can cause the nail to rip or tear out by the root.

Unlike cats, small furry pets cannot retract their nails. Clipping the nails on a regular basis will not only help prevent you from getting scratched, it will also protect the pet. Since trimming a small pet's nails can sometimes be difficult (and if done improperly, painful and traumatic) it is often best to have a veterinarian do it.

You can also have your veterinarian or a pet store employee show you how to trim your pet's nails so you can do it yourself. Use clippers designed for birds or cats and keep some styptic powder handy. The best time to trim the animal's nails is when he is tired, not when he is wide awake and playful. Two people are necessary, one to hold the pet, and one to clip the nails. A short cut is usually adequate, just enough to remove the sharp, pointed tip. The nail should not be cut below the quick (or vein area). If the nail is trimmed too short, it can cause painful bleeding, and the animal might bite if he is in pain.

Unlike those of cats, the claws of small furry pets are not retractable. Clipping them regularly will keep them from getting tangled in things and will prevent scratches.

Gentle, regular cleaning with a cotton swab will keep your small pet's ears clean and free of wax buildup.

EARS

Small animals can get ear mites and ear infections. If left untreated, these infestations can cause serious problems. Take your pet to a veterinarian if you notice excessive scratching, heavy wax buildup, discharge, or a growth.

Owners of rabbits should examine their pet's ears every few weeks. They can gently

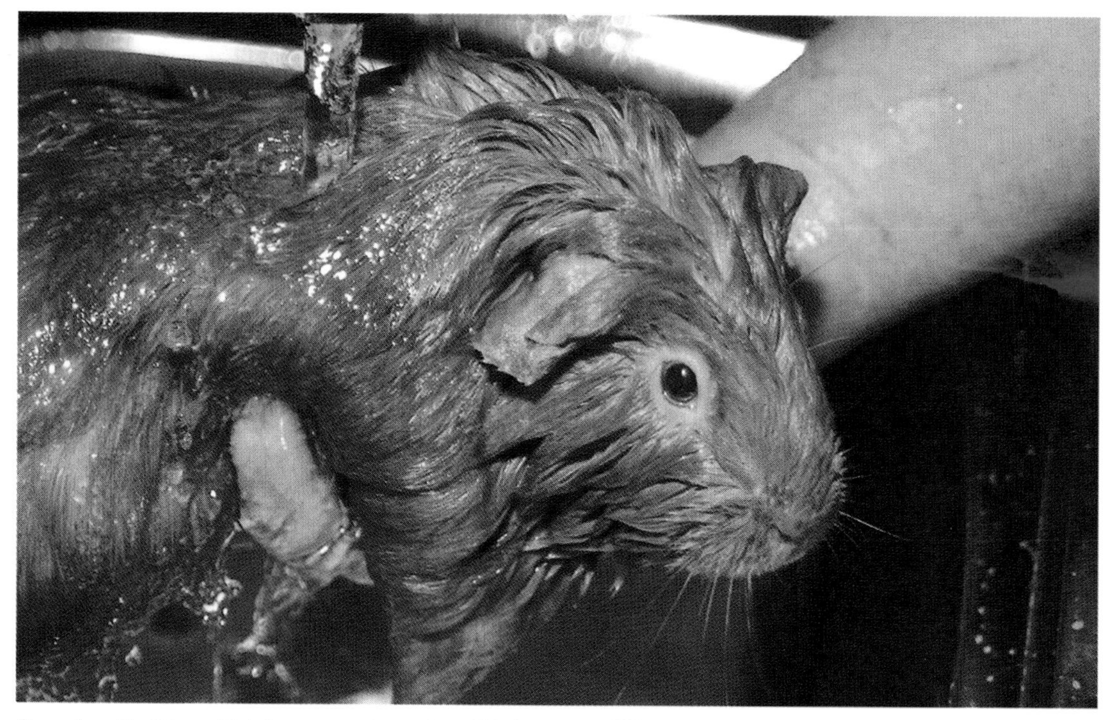

Occasional bathing with lukewarm water and a mild shampoo will keep your pet clean and odor-free.

Small animals should be dried with a soft towel immediately after their baths. Hair dryers can burn the animals' sensitive skin.

clean their pet's ears with a cotton swab and a veterinary ear cleanser. The wax in the external ear should be carefully removed, without going into the ear canal.

BATHING

Small animals generally do not need to be bathed. If a pet is dirty and smelly, it is usually because he has been lying on dirty bedding. Cleaning the cage, providing fresh, sweet-smelling bedding, and allowing the animal to groom himself is usually better than a bath. Nonetheless, pet owners who exhibit small animals in competitions do occasionally bathe them with lukewarm water and a mild shampoo. Immediately drying them with a towel is safest; hair dryers are not recommended because they can burn the animals' sensitive skin.

A Sick Pet

Small animals do not usually show symptoms of illness until late in the course of a disease. The ability to hide an illness is believed to be a self-protective behavior. In the wild, an animal that acts sick is an easy mark for predators. By the time a pet owner realizes that the animal is ill, the pet has usually been sick for quite some time. In many cases, treatment is difficult because the condition is so advanced at the time of detection.

Sick small animals generally present a similar range of symptoms. Obvious signs of illness include discharge from the eyes or nose. Sometimes the insides of an animal's front legs are dirty from wiping its nose. Sudden changes in behavior such as lethargy and reduced appetite can also indicate illness. Signs of disease that are more difficult to detect include rough hair, hunched posture, and weight loss.

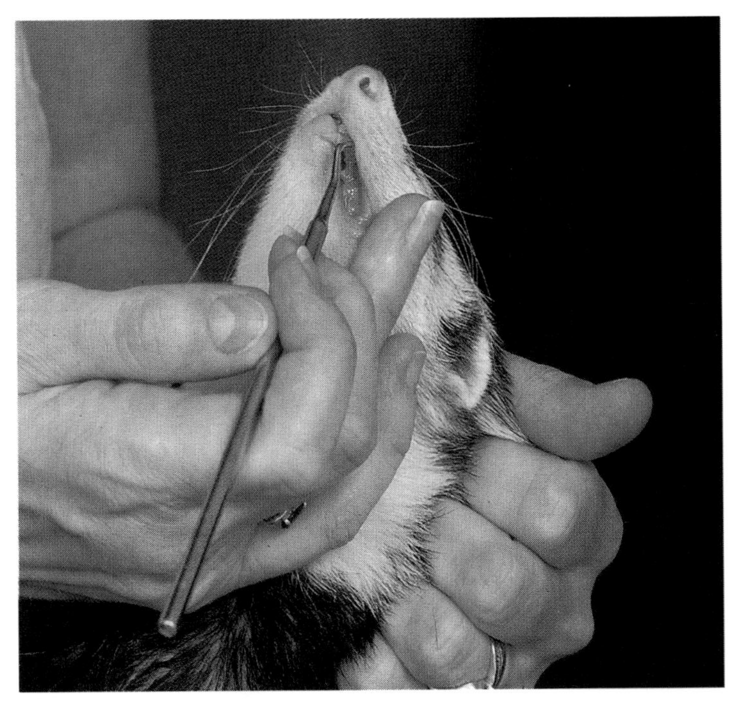

Dental health is important, too! Don't neglect your pet's regular teeth cleanings.

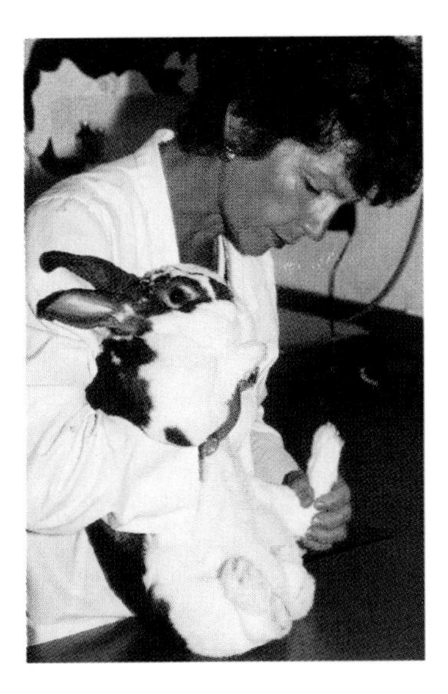

A visit to a veterinarian can be expensive, but it is the best chance for a cure if your pet is sick.

A visit to a veterinarian can be expensive, and many small animal owners (or the parents of a child with a small animal) find it difficult to spend large sums of money on a pet that might have cost only a few dollars. Even veterinarians often make "educated guesses" as to what ails the pet, because diagnostic tests can cost quite a bit. Pet stores sell some products that may be used for common illnesses, such as wet tail in hamsters. These treatments are options, but in general, a prompt visit to the veterinarian is the best guarantee of a successful outcome.

The ailments that affect small animals can be caused by a variety of things. Problems with small animals' feet, such as swollen feet or toes, are often the result of improper housing or keeping the animal on an irritating substrate. Since small pets often share a home, injuries from fighting can sometimes occur. After separating the animals, any wounds can be treated with a topical antibiotic. Tumors are a type of noninfectious disease that are seldom seen in young animals. More often, tumors occur in older animals. Small pets with tumors must be seen by a veterinarian to determine whether surgery is necessary.

Infectious diseases are caused by bacteria, viruses, and protozoans. Sometimes, the diseases caused by these agents are subclinical, meaning that signs of infection are difficult to detect. Individual animals also differ in their resistance to infectious organisms. Some exposed animals never display any symptoms. However, stress or other bacterial or viral

This unsightly condition is called bumblefoot and is extremely painful to the animal. Foot problems are common in small animals that are housed on wire mesh floors and other irritating surfaces or in dirty cages.

Overcrowding at large breeding farms and in pet stores can cause your new pet to arrive home sick and stressed out. A change in diet, temperature fluctuations, and a dirty environment can also cause stress and illness.

infections can cause an animal to suddenly show symptoms. An animal can experience stress when going to a new home, from a change in diet, exposure to temperature fluctuations, and so forth.

A clean cage is one of the most important ways to prevent a small animal from becoming ill. Poor husbandry is often the main reason that small pets become sick. Spoiled food and a dirty cage are invitations to illness. A clean, well-ventilated cage is essential, because the ammonia vapors from urine can irritate an animal's respiratory tract and allow diseases to develop or aggravate an existing illness.

Small animals often seem to tolerate a dirty environment. This trait is beneficial, since they frequently suffer from occasional neglect. They are hardy creatures, but their tolerance can eventually diminish and they will become ill if kept in an unsanitary environment.

Measures to prevent small animals from becoming sick are best. For example, a new pet should be quarantined from any pet(s) of the same species that you already have. Many people do not like the additional cost of buying another cage and supplies, and the chances of introducing an illness are not high if the new animal appears healthy and was obtained from a reliable source. Nonetheless, it is always safest to quarantine a new arrival to prevent the possible transmission of an illness to an already beloved pet. Two to three weeks is usually sufficient.

It is very important to quarantine a new arrival for a few weeks to make sure he is healthy before introducing him to your other pets of the same species.

Training

Training your pet to perform a trick can be fun. Most owners enjoy the challenge, and many small pets enjoy the attention. Perhaps you have seen a rat trained to walk a tightrope or a rabbit that walks on a leash and wondered how to train your own pet.

Keep in mind that certain types of small animals are easier to train than others. Rats, for example, are considered the smartest small animal. Because of their agility, species such as mice and rats can be trained to do more interesting tricks than guinea pigs, for example, which are not very agile. In addition, some pets are calmer than others and so are more easily trained. A timid, easily frightened pet is difficult to train.

Your pet must be tame before you can train him. A tame pet will let you hold and pick him up without becoming frightened. Ideally, your pet will be comfortable in a variety of situations. The more time you spend holding and playing with your pet, the more quickly he will learn to trust you and become tame. A pet that is handled frequently is easier to train than one that is left by itself for long periods of time.

Once your pet is tame, you can decide what you want to train him to do. You should base your decision on your pet's natural abilities and behaviors. For example, animals such as gerbils and mice stand up to smell the air or investigate new situations, and they can be taught to stand up and walk on their hind feet for a treat. However, a guinea pig lacks the necessary dexterity and cannot be taught this. He can, however, learn to come when called. Watch your pet when you let him out of his cage to play. You might notice

Rats are both smart and agile, making it easy to teach them interesting tricks such as rope-climbing or tightrope-walking.

Base your trick training on your pet's natural behaviors. For example, if your hamster loves to swing on the monkey bars, teach him to do it for a treat.

Guinea pigs are less dexterous than hamsters, but both species are trained the same way.

some natural ability, such as jumping, that you can then develop into a trick.

To train your pet you will use a process called "the method of approximation," or "shaping." You will shape your pet's behavior by rewarding behaviors that are close to the behavior you want. A brief review of the basic principles of this method will help you get started.

You will use a reward of food to change and reinforce your pet's behavior—for example, when your gerbil stands up, and then later, when it moves forward a few steps on its hind legs. You should also say the command "up" to your pet. Small animal treats or pieces of dry cereal are good for this purpose. Always give your pet a very small piece of the treat. If you give your pet a piece that is too large, he will quickly fill up and will no longer respond to your training attempts.

You must give your pet the food reward immediately after he has done what you wanted him to do. Your pet must be able to make the connection between the food reward and his action. Petting and enthusiastic praise also work for some animals, but your pet will perform more consistently if he receives a food reward.

Suppose you want to train your pet to come when called. Training your pet to come when called works best in a small area that your pet has already explored where there is nothing frightening or new to investigate. First, let your pet play in and become familiar with the pet-safe room where you will be training him. Let your pet begin his explorations with you sitting on the ground. Start by placing your pet a few inches from where you are sitting. Call your pet's name and reward him with food if he comes to you. Slowly increase the distance your pet must move to come back to you, always rewarding your pet. Be reasonable about the distance you expect your pet to respond from. A rat or rabbit might travel several yards when called. However, a mouse or hamster is most likely to respond when only a few inches away.

After your pet has learned a given behavior, you should stop giving him food each time he does what you want, and instead, randomly reward him with a food treat. Your pet will work harder to try to get a reward of food when you reinforce the learned behavior at random. Do not train your pet for more than a couple of ten-minute sessions each day.

Always end on a positive note—even when your pet has done only one small thing well. Avoid the temptation to make your pet work too hard for too long.

If you want your pet to perform tricks in front of an audience, you must also train him in an area where other people and distractions are, such as the living room. If you only train your pet in a quiet room, your pet is likely to get frightened and distracted if you later try to have him perform for friends and family.

BODY LANGUAGE

Knowing your pet's body language can help you be more sensitive to your pet's moods and help you to train your pet better. You do not want to continue a training session if your pet becomes scared.

When frightened, your pet might run away, kick, bite, scratch, or lie flat on the ground and freeze. As part of the "flight or fight response," some frightened animals defecate. Sometimes, nervous small animals rapidly groom themselves. If your pet exhibits any of these behaviors, you should talk gently to him, then put him back into his house so that he can calm down.

Knowing your pet's body language can help you be more sensitive to your pet's moods and help you train your pet better.

Tricks don't have to be entertaining—they can be practical, too. For example, ferrets can be trained to ride quietly in a tote bag you carry over your shoulder.

Many small pets, such as guinea pigs and rats, spring, leap, and twist in the air when happy. The sound of gentle tooth grinding can indicate contentment in many small pets, such as rabbits and rats. Loud tooth grinding is usually heard from two animals before they fight. Preceding a fight, small animals with long tails often wag their tails back and forth. When curious, both gerbils and rabbits will stand up on their hind legs, ears alert, noses twitching, to investigate their surroundings.

Suggested Reading

RE 502
The Guide to Owning a Ferret
Mary Field
64 pages, more than 70 full-color photos

RE 504
The Guide to Owning a Guinea Pig
Graham J. Edsel
64 pages, 55 full-color photos

RE 507
The Guide to Owning a Rabbit
Anne Lindsay
64 pages, more than 70 full-color photos

RE 505
The Guide to Owning a Hamster
Anmarie Barrie
64 pages, more than 55 full-color photos

RE 503
The Guide to Owning a Gerbil
Perry Putman
64 pages, 55 full-color photos

RE 506
The Guide to Owning a Mouse
Howard Hirschhorn
64 pages, more than 50 full-color photos

RE 508
The Guide to Owning a Rat
Susan Fox
64 pages, 40 full-color photos